HEAVEN QUEST

A Detour Home

JOSHUA LEDESMA

ISBN 978-1-63575-158-1 (Paperback)
ISBN 978-1-63575-159-8 (Digital)

Copyright © 2017 by Joshua Ledesma
All rights reserved. No part of this publication may be reproduced, distributed, or transmitted in any form or by any means, including photocopying, recording, or other electronic or mechanical methods without the prior written permission of the publisher. For permission requests, solicit the publisher via the address below.

Christian Faith Publishing, Inc.
296 Chestnut Street
Meadville, PA 16335
www.christianfaithpublishing.com

Printed in the United States of America

Contents

Introduction..5

Part 1: The Past (Where You've Been)

    Chapter 1: One Simple Don't 11

    Chapter 2: Easily Deceived 18

    Chapter 3: Drawn to Sin......................................25

    Chapter 4: A Follower of Sin................................30

    Chapter 5: Leaders in Sin....................................42

    Chapter 6: The Wrong Destination 50

Part 2: The Present (Where You Are)

    Chapter 7: Changing Direction (Repentance)................59

    Chapter 8: Where to Go from There (Born Again) 66

    Chapter 9: Like a Newborn Baby..............................74

    Chapter 10: With Opened Eyes (We Call It Mud)............83

    Chapter 11: Learn from the Best.................................94

    Chapter 12: Is Sunday Church Enough? 122

Chapter 13: Unless You Try 129
Chapter 14: The Greatest of These 145
Chapter 15: A Ticket Home 154
Chapter 16: The Formula 166
Chapter 17: The Compass 174

INTRODUCTION

Where are you from? You could tell me any city, state, or country in the world, and I'd look at you and simply say, "I'm sorry, but I believe you are wrong." Philippians 3:20 out of the NLT version of the Bible reads, " But we are citizens of heaven, where the Lord Jesus Christ lives. And we are eagerly waiting for him to return as our Savior."

So let me ask this again. Where are you from? If you said, "Heaven," I'd say, "Welcome to planet Earth." So it appears to me that man was created in heaven, and God intended man to live in heaven forever, but now we have to sort of earn our way back to heaven.

Rick Warren says that earth is a temporary assignment, and here is where we are preparing for what we are going to be doing in heaven. It's not my intention to tell you what exactly heaven really is and exactly how it's going to be; the intention of this book is more to help you get there.

Right now we are on planet Earth, but our destination is heaven. What is the best way to figure out how to get from one place to another if you have no memory of getting there before? I suppose some of you may say "GPS," or perhaps, "Ask someone else," but what I'm going to recommend is something I like to call a "map."

If you showed me an actual map and asked me what it was, I'm 99 percent positive I could confidently tell you that it was a map, and

I'd be right. When I decided to use the word *map* to describe what my book's intention is, I decided to do a little research on what a map truly is, what its main purposes are, and what its top uses are.

I believe that learning what a map truly is will help you understand how to get the most out of this book. Before I tell you what I researched, I want to you stop for just a moment and think about this simple question: What is the purpose of a map? Now I want to ask this question: What are maps used for? Now think about this: Were your answers the same?

I looked up the purpose of maps, and this was my top answer: "Maps allow people to understand their place in the world." Let me highlight something there. Maps allow people to *understand their place* in the world. Now here are a few little facts about maps. Maps have become more accurate over time. Maps allowed navigators to reach distant locations. Determining how to make a world map is difficult because the earth is round, and any flat map contains distortions.

I then looked up what maps are used for. To my surprise, the answers were not exactly the same. A map is used to find out how to get somewhere. A map is used to look over a particular state or country. A map is used to show you where things are. Let me tell you what I picture a map being used for. I'm big on camping and the outdoors, and I believe a map would be great for helping start a fire. Other than that, I've never really used one.

I remember growing up going on long car rides and trying to look at a map. They made no sense to me, and by the time I was old enough to need to use one by myself, they had come out with GPS, which is something I use quite often. But a GPS is basically someone else telling you how to get where you are going.

One time, I was sent to another city for work, and my boss gave me the address of the place I was headed, so I typed it into my GPS and started on my trip. As I got closer and closer, I began looking for the building. I ended up crossing some railroad tracks, and when the only thing in front of me was a field, the GPS kept saying, "Arriving at destination on right." Can you imagine my frustration? I ended up getting there only after stopping at a convenience store, asking for help, and drawing a small map to help me get there. I'll now make two statements that I believe best describe the similarity between what a map means to the world and navigation, and what this book means to your chances of making it to heaven. A map tells you where you've been, where you are, and where you're going to be. The last thing I want to tell you about maps before I begin to show you the map is this: maps were neither discovered nor invented; they emerged out of a necessity. Highlight that word—*necessity!*

Up to a certain point in our lives, we've just become something, or someone. We learned everything we know from someone else who then either consciously, or possibly without even knowing it, taught us something. Unfortunately, what they taught us may or may not have been a good, positive thing. This book was designed to show the journey we begin from the time we are born into this world.

Some of us are born into millionaire families, some to what the world calls middle class, and the unfortunate fact of the matter is that some are born into a Dumpster. Some have two biological parents, some have one, and some have none. Some have two great adoptive parents, some have none. Everyone is born into a different life, but we are all born into the same world, a world full of sin.

From the time we are born, we learn simple things like untying our shoes to take them off or put them on, but once they are on, we tie them to secure them to our foot. Kids are thrilled when they learn to tie their own shoes, but then comes a day when they learn they don't have to tie or untie them at all. After seeing their friend or sibling just slip off their shoe without first untying it, that's all it took to undo what their parents had taught them. That same example can be used in a million different ways.

We begin to learn the right things, and then we begin to learn the wrong things, which usually overshadow what we've previously learned. So what does it take to get back to the basics? What does it take to be "born again"? Something very important that Jesus says is, unless you are "born again," you can't enter the kingdom of heaven. Hopefully, I'll help to make that clear very soon.

While I was writing this book, I began to deeply think about whether this book would really make a difference. One day, as I felt I was getting close to finishing this book, I was having a conversation with myself about the importance of this book, and Satan decided to throw his two cents in. He said that if Jesus couldn't reach certain people, "why do you think you can?" And instantly, I thought he made a very good point. But then I could hear God's words, plain and simple, the words Jesus spoke in John 14:12: "Verily, verily I say unto you, He that believeth on me, the works that I shall do he do also; and greater works than these shall he do; because I go unto my Father."

From that moment on, I've felt more than confident in the message I'm going to be pouring out to you in this book. I hope you find it interesting, helpful, and mind-changing. These words are taken out of Romans 12:2: "But ye be transformed by the renewing of your mind." I can't change the world, and I can't change your life, but if enough people can change their mind and then their lives, the world will begin to change for the better. There are many other books out there to help change minds, but no other book has the exact message I'm going to be sending throughout the rest of this book.

PART 1

The Past (Where You've Been)

They say that life comes down to a series of moments, and in those moments are choices; decisions we make that could affect our lives forever. We were in one of the worst fights we've ever been in but all I could think about; I mean the one thing that kept echoing in my mind was how, how did we get here.
—Tristan, *Bluehill Avenue*

It doesn't matter where you've been, it's where you are now, and the direction in which you are headed.

CHAPTER 1

ONE SIMPLE DON'T

Don't die! From the moment your parents know of your existence, they only have one thing they ask of you: "Please don't die." From the moment you enter this world, you are helpless. Under the care of, first, the doctor and medical staff, and then it's on to your parents. They have to feed you, clean you, clothe you, etc. They are expected to teach you the basics of life and get you enrolled in school where you'll begin to learn from others. With that said, your parents still have the responsibility of getting you up, making sure you're fed, dressed properly, have everything you need, and getting you to school.

What comes next will be discussed in further chapters, but the point I'm trying to make is, up to a certain point in life, you need others to make sure you are able to mature properly; but when you are firstborn, you are basically helpless with one expectation. Don't die. After God made man and placed him in the Garden of Eden, he gave him one "don't" command. He said he could eat of every tree, but don't eat of the tree of knowledge of good and evil, for in that day, he would surely die. Genesis 2:15–17 reads,

> And the Lord God took the man and put him into the garden of Eden to dress it and to keep it. And the Lord God commanded the man, saying, Of every tree of the garden thou mayest freely eat: but of the tree of the knowledge of good and evil, thou shalt not eat of it: for in the day that thou eatest thereof thou shalt surely die.

Doesn't it almost sound like God is simply saying, "Don't die"? Now, there is a major difference between us as newborn babies and Adam at the time of his "one simple don't." Adam had no one to do for him and show him how to live. All he was told to do was "be fruitful and multiply," which he did, but it wasn't long before God realized man needed to be told a few more don't commands.

The Ten Commandments

In Exodus chapter 20, God decided it was time to give humanity a few more commands. What I find amazing is that God still doesn't really tell humans how to live in a way that pleases him, at least not specifically. Exodus 20:3 begins the Ten Commandments. Of the Ten Commandments, eight of these are don't commands, leaving only two for telling us what to do; and they are in no way, shape, or form specific as to how to live. Let's take a look at Exodus 20:1–17:

> And God spake all these words, saying, I am the Lord thy God, which have brought thee out of the land of Egypt, out of the house of bondage. Thou shalt have no other gods before me. Thou shalt not make unto thee any graven image,

or any likeness of anything that is in heaven above, or that is in the earth beneath, or that is in the water under the earth: thou shalt not bow down thyself to them, nor serve them: for I the Lord thy God am a jealous God, visiting the iniquity of the fathers upon the children unto the third and fourth generation of them that hate me; and showing mercy unto thousands of them that love me, and keep my commandments. Thou shalt not take the name of the Lord thy God in vain; for the Lord will not hold him guiltless that taketh his name in vain. Remember the Sabbath day, to keep it holy. Six days shalt thou labor, and do all thy work: but the seventh day is the Sabbath of the Lord thy God: in it thou shalt not do any work, thou, nor thy son, nor thy manservant, nor thy maidservant, nor thy cattle, nor thy stranger that is within thy gates: for in six days the Lord made heaven and earth, the sea, and all that in them is, and rested the seventh day: wherefore the Lord blessed the Sabbath day, and hallowed it. Honour thy father and thy mother: that thy days may be long upon the land which the Lord thy God giveth thee. Thou shalt not kill. Thou shalt not commit adultery. Thou shalt not steal. Thou shalt not bear false witness against thy neighbor. Thou shalt not covet thy neighbour's house, thou shalt not covet thy neighbour's wife, nor his manservant, nor his maidservant, nor his ox, nor his ass, nor any thing that is thy neighbor's.

So when God was speaking to Adam, the man whom he formed from the dust of the ground and into whose nostrils he breathed the breath of life and placed him in the Garden of Eden, God was telling him two things: one, don't eat of the tree of knowledge of good and evil; and two, be fruitful and multiply. Now he comes out with this. Everything he said in verses 3–17 is summed up into the following:

1. You shall have no other gods before me.
2. You shall not make idols.
3. You shall not take the name of the Lord your God in vain.
4. Remember the Sabbath day, to keep it holy.
5. Honor your father and your mother.
6. You shall not murder.
7. You shall not commit adultery.
8. You shall not steal.
9. You shall not bear false witness against your neighbor.
10. You shall not covet.

A World Gone Wrong

So what inspired this new list of commands that God has now given? Let's take a look at a few events that took place between the time of God's first two commands and what he said in Exodus chapter 20, which is summed up into eight commands about what not do and two commands of what to do.

Genesis chapter 4 begins with evidence that Adam was following through with carrying out God's first command of what to do: be fruitful and multiply.

> And Adam knew Eve his wife; and she conceived, and bare Cain, and said, I have gotten

a man from the Lord. And she again bare his brother Abel.

Seven verses after Cain's birth, he was violating God's sixth commandment. But this was long before the command was ever given. Genesis 4:8 reads,

And Cain talked with Abel his brother: and it came to pass, when they were in the field, that Cain rose up against his brother, and slew him.

That was only the beginning of evil on earth. Genesis 6:5 reads,

And God saw that the wickedness of man was great in the earth, and that every imagination of the thoughts of his heart was only evil continually. And it repented the Lord that he had made man on the earth, and it grieved him at his heart.

Now, it doesn't tell us much about what exactly man was doing that made God want to destroy his creation in which Genesis 1:31 says, "And God saw everything that he made, and behold, it was very good." God looked upon his creation and saw that one man, and one man only, was living in a way that pleased him. Only problem is, we know almost nothing about how exactly Noah was living. All we know is that he was married and had three children who were also married. So what we know about him is that he was a family man. He was obeying God's first "do" command of being fruitful and multiplying.

After God flooded the earth and repopulated it using Noah and his family, it is almost amazing how quickly things seemed to have returned right back to the wickedness God saw, which the Bible describes as having "grieved him at his heart." First of all, let's look at Noah, a man whom Genesis 6:9 describes as "a just man and perfect in his generations." Genesis 9:20–25 reads,

> And Noah began to be a husbandman, and he planted a vineyard: and he drank of the wine, and was drunken; and he was uncovered within his tent. And Ham, the father of Canaan, saw the nakedness of his father, and told his two brethren without. And Shem and Japheth took a garment, and laid it upon both their shoulders, and went backward, and covered the nakedness of their father; and their faces were backward, and they saw not their father's nakedness. And Noah awoke from his wine, and knew what his younger son had done unto him. And he said, Cursed be Canaan; a servant of servants shall he be unto his brethren.

Now I seriously doubt that when God was looking around the world—seeing the wickedness that grieved his heart and seeing Noah in a similar situation, passed out drunk from wine he was by nobody else forced to drink, waking up and cursing his grandson—God was thinking to himself something along the lines of, *There, that guy! That guy is perfect! If everyone was like him, the world would once again be pleasing to me. I'm going to destroy everyone except that guy.* This is only the beginning of unbelievable events that display many of the same character defects that can easily be pinpointed in humans today. After this, we see anything from lying to murder. But a few things that can't quite be described in one word are acts such as brothers stealing from each other, wives telling their husband to do what we now consider committing adultery, sisters getting their father drunk to sleep with them, men telling their wives to pose as their sister. Among the other acts we find in the book of Genesis are rape and various forms of deceit, which include false accusations of rape that landed an innocent man in prison. So how did the world or, more specifically, how did humans stray so far from what God had thought of when he created man? Well, it's very simple. It's a word I just mentioned for the first time two sentences back. Man was deceived.

Chapter 2

Easily Deceived

Humans are supposed to be the most intelligent beings on earth. In Genesis 1:26, God decided to make man and "let them have dominion over the fish of the sea, and over the fowl of the air, and over the cattle, and over all the earth, and over every creeping thing that creepeth upon the earth." But humans have one major downfall. From the beginning of time, humans, for some reason, are very easily deceived. Genesis 2:15–17 reads,

> And the Lord God took the man, and put him into the garden of Eden to dress it and to keep it. And the Lord God commanded the man, saying, Of every tree of the garden thou mayest freely eat: for in the day that thou eatest thereof thou shalt surely die.

Now it appeared that man was doing just fine at obeying God's command—until man was deceived, that is. Genesis chapter 3 begins with the serpent approaching Eve, preparing to deceive her. It doesn't ever say that God told Eve specifically not to eat of the tree, as he actually told Adam before he even took Eve from one of Adams ribs, but it's very clear that she knew she wasn't supposed to eat of the tree. Genesis 3:2–4 reads,

> And the woman said unto the serpent, We may eat of the fruit of the trees of the garden: but of the fruit of the tree which is in the midst of the garden, God hath said, Ye shall not eat of it, neither shall ye touch it, lest ye die. And the serpent said unto the woman, Ye shall not surely die.

All it took was the serpent coming along and telling Eve it was okay to do something, and all of a sudden, Eve viewed the tree in a completely different way. Genesis 3:6 reads,

> And when the woman saw that the tree was good for food, and that it was pleasant to the eyes, and a tree to be desired to make one wise, she took of the fruit thereof, and did eat, and gave also unto her husband with her; and he did it.

God only gave one command of what not to do, but all it took was someone else telling him it was okay and doing it with him for Adam to do exactly what God told him not to do. Now let's look at how Adam responds to God when questioned about his act of disobedience. After Adam and Eve hid themselves because of their nakedness, God asked Adam who told him he was naked and asked if he had eaten of the tree that he commanded him that he could not eat of. Genesis 3:12 reads,

> And the man said, The woman whom thou gavest to be with me, she gave me of the tree, and I did eat.

In the following verse, Eve makes sure to point out that she didn't come up with this plan all on her own. She was beguiled by the serpent. Can you remember the first time you did something you'd been told you weren't supposed to do? If you're human, you probably tried pushing the blame on someone else, most likely the person who peer-pressured you into doing it, or possibly even blaming an imaginary person to protect the real identity of the person who, in fact, did deceive you. Adam's response was classic. Already being caught, he openly admitted that, yes, he did in fact disobey God's command, but look whom he actually pushed the blame on. It wasn't just Eve who handed him the fruit, he said. The woman whom God gave him gave him the fruit. So he basically blamed God. Never did Adam blame the serpent who, in fact, caused the whole thing. Now let's look at why man was so easily deceived.

God didn't give a lot of reasons for why he didn't want Adam and Eve to eat of the tree, but he gave them one consequence: "for in that day, you would surely die." All it took was the serpent taking away that one consequence, and that changed everything. How often is the reason for us not doing something because we don't want the consequences that come with it? When Eve ate of the fruit, she was convinced that it was okay to eat of it. She had no idea what was going to come next. She gave the fruit to Adam, who ate with her. When their eyes were opened, they weren't dancing because they had just received some great new ability in which they thought to themselves, *Why didn't we do this sooner?* They hid in shame from their nakedness. After that, they were cast from the Garden of Eden to till the ground in which man was taken. They were both cursed. God cursed the ground for Adam's sake, and for the woman, he greatly multiplied her sorrow during childbirth. God never mentioned any of these things when he told man not to eat of the fruit.

Unexpected Deceivers

Here is another scenario where someone was told they'd get away with something without consequences, which was very clearly not the case. Genesis chapter 27 begins with Isaac growing old and feeling it was time for him to bless his oldest son before he died. He told his oldest son, Esau, "I know not the day of my death: now therefore take, I pray thee, thy weapons, thy quiver and thy bow, and go out to the field, and take me some venison; and make me savory meat such as I love, and bring it to me, that I may eat; that my soul may bless thee before I die."

Unfortunately for Esau, who was about to receive his blessing from his father and after already being forced to choose between his life or selling his birthright for a single meal, his mother had other plans. Rebekah, who loved Esau's younger brother, Jacob, more than her older son, overheard the conversation between Isaac and Esau. Rebekah told Jacob that she heard Isaac tell Esau he was going to bless him before he died and then came up with a plan of her own. Genesis 27:8–10 reads,

> Now therefore, my son, obey my voice according to that which I command thee. Go now to the flock, and fetch me from thence two good kids of the goats; and I will make them savoury meat for thy father, such as he loveth; and thou shalt bring it to thy father, that he may eat, and that he may bless thee before his death.

Jacob actually seemed to almost have avoided going through with this deception, until he himself was deceived by his own mother. We just looked at how man was deceived by his wife, who was deceived by a serpent. Now we're about to see how a young man was deceived by his own mother. Verses 11 and 12 are Jacob pointing out that his brother was a hairy man and his skin was smooth and that he would appear to his father as a deceiver and that would bring a curse upon him, not a blessing. But his mother fired back with this. Genesis 27:13 reads,

> And his mother said unto him, upon me be thy curse, my son: only obey my voice, and go fetch me them.

The main story here is how Jacob deceived his father and brother as he posed as Esau to steal his blessing. They actually went through quite the trouble to deceive Isaac. First of all, he was being deceived by his own wife and child; and to do so, his wife had to come up with quite the plan. She sent her son to get some of their own flock while Esau was out hunting for wild game. She then had to cover Jacob with the skins of the goats in which he used for the meat to feed his father. Even then, Isaac felt something just wasn't quite right. He knew Jacob had returned with the meat a little faster than what he expected Esau to return with the venison he ordered, but luckily for Jacob and Rebekah, Isaac truly believed that God could do anything. Genesis 27:20 reads,

> And Isaac said unto his son, How is it that thou hast found it so quickly, my son? And he said, Because the Lord thy God brought it to me.

If it wasn't for Isaac's faith in God, they very well could have been caught right there as they obviously didn't want to wait a reasonable amount of time, not wanting to chance Esau getting back too soon. After that, he continued to test Jacob through skepticism and felt him and said that the voice was of Jacob but the hands were Esau's. But with all that said, Isaac continued on and blessed Jacob. Remember, Jacob was hesitant to go through with this plan at first, saying he might be cursed instead of blessed, and her mother simply said that she would take any punishment that he may receive. Rebekah actually prodded him to do what he obviously knew was wrong and convinced him to go through with it by telling him there would be no consequences.

After Esau found out that the same brother who already made him sell him his birthright for a single meal had now also stolen his blessing, he then decides that he would kill Jacob, but not until the day of his father's death. As soon as Rebekah heard these words, she devised another plan to get Jacob out of the presence of Esau and had Jacob sent to her brother, Laban, in Haran. Almost immediately, you can see small signs of a curse, or at least some sort of consequences as Jacob had to sleep on the ground using a stone for a pillow. He then ended up working for Laban for twenty years, in which he said that Laban changed his wages ten times. Genesis 31:41 reads,

> Thus have I been twenty years in thy house; I served thee fourteen years for thy two daughters, and six years for thy cattle: and thou hast changed my wages ten times.

So if we sum up the events that took place after Jacob stole Esau's blessing, in which his mother told him she would take on any curse that may be given, Jacob was forced to leave his home, in which he then had to sleep on the ground using a stone for a pillow. He then began to work for his uncle, by whom he was deceived as he agreed to work seven years for Rachel but was given Leah instead. Jacob then agreed to work another seven years for what he had already worked seven years for. Eventually fleeing from Laban, who pursued him, Jacob headed home, somewhere he also didn't feel safe. He then had to send gifts ahead, basically begging for his brother's mercy. It doesn't quite seem as if he got off without consequences or a curse. So how and why are humans so easily deceived? If you didn't know any better, you'd think humans were without a choice, simply drawn to sin.

Chapter 3
Drawn to Sin

Isn't it amazing how something so wrong can look and sound so good? Eve saw the fruit she was not supposed to eat as "pleasant to the eyes." David viewed Bathsheba, the married woman whom he had an affair with and whose husband he had killed to cover his sin as "very beautiful to look upon." When Abram and Lot separated, Lot chose to dwell in Sodom because of how the land appeared. Genesis 13:10 includes the words, "And Lot lifted up his eyes, and beheld all the plain of Jordan, that it was well watered every where."

Also, let's consider the idols that were being worshipped. When the Israelites began to complain to Aaron after Moses's absence while he was talking to God, they asked for gods to worship and willingly gave up their gold jewelry for Aaron to build them a golden calf. It's safe to say that the golden calf was probably a little easier to look upon than just a simple wooden cross.

What Are We Fighting For?

It's amazing how much we are actually willing to do to get what we want and how little we will do just to do the right thing. We'll do the right thing if it's convenient, but it's safe to say that since the beginning of time, humans put more effort into sin than into righteousness. If you ask multiple different people what the definition of the word *champion* is, I'm sure you would get several different responses. My favorite definition is "someone who fights for a cause."

In 1 Samuel chapter 17, when the Israelites and the Philistines were awaiting battle, both armies standing on opposite mountains separated by only a valley between them, the Bible says that a champion arose. This verse, 1 Samuel 17:4, has rubbed me the wrong way ever since I read a book about a man of God who did something so incredible it earned him a spot as the sixteenth book in the Holy Bible: Nehemiah.

The problem with the champion spoken of in the Bible is he did not fight for God. The Bible was referring to Goliath, a man who defied the army that David referred to as "the armies of the living God" in 1 Samuel 17:26. Most people consider a champion someone who wins. Unless the Bible is mistaken, a champion isn't necessarily the man who "wins"! Now, with that said, who wouldn't want to be known as a champion? Who wouldn't want to *be* a champion? So let me make this very clear. Whether you win or lose, whether you succeed or fail, you can be a champion. All you have to do is fight for a cause. I'd like to think we all fight for something, but are we fighting for the right things?

I'd like to point out something in 1 Genesis 3:6: "And when the woman saw that the tree was good for food, *and* that it was pleasant to the eyes, *and* a tree to be desired to make one wise" (italics added). Notice the *and*s. Once we have our eyes set on something, we'll justify it any way we can. We can come up with as many excuses as we want to justify doing what we have been told not to do. If we didn't, in some way, think it was wrong or that someone whose opinion we care about wouldn't approve of what we are doing, we wouldn't feel the need to give multiple reasons for doing something. When we have to give multiple reasons for what we are doing, we are trying to justify our actions. And if it's not as easy as simply doing it, we'll do whatever is necessary to do it.

David Pursues Sin

Look how much trouble David went through to have what he set his eyes on in 2 Samuel 11:2. First he sent messengers to find out more about Bathsheba. The reports came back with news that should have stopped David from any further plans to have what he had already set his eyes on. Verse 3 says, "And one said, is not this Bathsheba, the daughter of Eliam, the wife of Uriah the Hittite?" From the time David heard that she was married, he should have been able to recall the seventh commandment and not committed adultery. But it was too late; he was already locked into his sin. It was almost like he was drawn to her without a choice. He sent for her and lay with her. She then sent and told David that she would be having his child. David obviously knew what he did was very wrong because he then went through great lengths to cover his sin. David tried to send Uriah back to his house so that he could lie with his wife and the baby could be passed off as his own, therefore covering up David's sin. When Uriah refused to go home, David had him thrown into the front lines of battle to be killed. Second Samuel 11:14–15 reads,

> And it came to pass in the morning, that David wrote a letter to Joab, and sent it by the hand of Uriah. And he wrote in the letter, saying, Set ye Uriah in the forefront of the hottest battle, and retire ye from him, that he may be smitten, and die.

The closing words of verse 17 are, "And Uriah the Hittite died also." David had now disobeyed commandment number six; on top of which, from the moment he received news that Bathsheba was married, he also began disobeying number ten as well. The closing sentence of chapter 11 reads as follows: "But the thing that David had done displeased the Lord." Let's now look at how God handled this. Chapter 12 begins with the prophet Nathan being sent to David. Second Samuel Chapter 12:1–7 reads,

> And the Lord sent Nathan unto David. And he came unto him, and said unto him, There were two men in one city; the one rich, and the other poor. The rich man had exceeding many flocks and herds: but the poor man had nothing, save one little ewe lamb, which he had bought and nourished up: and it grew up together with him, and with his children; it did eat of his own meat, and drank of his own cup, and lay in his bosom, and was unto him as a daughter. And there came a traveler unto the rich man, and he spared to take of his own flock and of his own herd, to dress for the wayfaring man that was come unto him; but took the poor man's lamb, and dressed it for the man that was come to him. And David's anger was greatly kindled against the man; and he said to Nathan, As the Lord liveth, the man that hath done this thing shall surely die: and he shall restore the lamb fourfold, because he did this thing, and because he had no pity. And Nathan said to David, Thou art the man.

David knew that he sinned, but he thought he had kept his sin covered up. God made sure David knew that he couldn't hide anything from him and that his sin wouldn't be unpunished. Second Samuel 12:12–13 reads,

> For thou didst it secretly: but I will do this thing before all Israel, and before the sun. And David said unto Nathan, I have sinned against the Lord.

So if David knew that what he was doing was wrong, why did he do it? Well, I guess you have to ask yourself why you do something that you've been told was wrong. Let's sum up what really took place here: David saw a beautiful woman bathing. At that time, he knew nothing about her. Had she not been married already, he could have simply made her his wife and went on living life without sin; but once he laid eyes on her, there was no reason good enough to change his mind about her. He sent for her, found out that she was married, but went ahead and slept with her anyway. He then received news that she was bearing his child and tried to pass it off as Uriah's, but when that wasn't possible, he had him killed. Then David married Bathsheba. He thought he was in the clear, but God sent a prophet to tell him that his sin was not unnoticed. David felt his punishment should be death, but God said not to worry, for he would not die, but his son would. David set his mind on something, and even though more obstacles kept getting in his way, it never stopped David. For him, it wasn't as simple as grabbing a piece of fruit and taking a bite; he actually had to pursue his sin. I'm now going to point out something very disturbing. It's no wonder that these sins, or what lead to these sins, were described as "beautiful." Look how Satan is described in Ezekiel 28:12: "full of wisdom and perfect in beauty." Now, I'm sure everyone reading this is guilty of pursuing sin, but what is more common is simply following in it.

CHAPTER 4

A FOLLOWER OF SIN

Genesis 19:31–35 begins with Lot and his two daughters staying in a cave just after God sent angels to destroy Sodom and Gomorrah because of their wickedness. Lot's family was spared only after Abraham pleaded to God for his nephew's sake. Lot and his family were told to run for their life and not to look back. Lot's wife didn't heed the advice of the angels, for Genesis 19:26 reads,

But his wife looked back from behind him, and she became a pillar of salt.

Also noted is the fact that Lot's daughters' husbands didn't listen, for verse 14 reads,

> And Lot went out, and spake unto his sons in law, which married his daughters, and said, Up, get you out of this place; for the Lord will destroy this city. But he seemed as one that mocked unto his sons in law.

Did She Really Just Say That?

This left his daughters without child and seemingly no one to help them carry on the name of their father. What is absolutely befuddling is how Lot's daughters proceeded to go about this conundrum. Genesis 19:31–35 reads:

> And the firstborn said unto the younger, Our father is old, and there is not a man in the earth to come in unto us after the manner of all the earth: come, let us make our father drink wine, and we will lie with him, that we may preserve seed of our father. And they made their father drink wine that night; and the firstborn went in, and lay with their father; and he perceived not when she lay down, nor when she arose. And it came to pass on the morrow, that the firstborn said unto the younger, Behold, I lay yesternight with my father: let us make him drink wine this night also; and go thou in, and lie with him, that we may preserve seed of our father. And they made their father drink wine that night also: and the younger arose, and lay with him; and he perceived not when she lay down, nor when she arose.

Now, if I were including sarcasm in this book, I'd use it right now and say something like, "Older daughter of Lot, you are a genius. Absolutely brilliant, I say! You will be making every important decision for humans everywhere from this point on. You are a marvelous thinker, absolutely incredible are you." But since I'm not, I'm going to say something more along the lines of, "Can you believe how she decided to handle that situation? And that she not only decided to perform an incredible sin but then went on to have her younger sister follow in her footsteps, footsteps that led right to a strangely constructed ball of sin?" I'd like to first look at this from the younger daughter's perspective.

Here she was, just had to flee from her home, which was destroyed for its wickedness; now she was staying in a cave with her older sister and dad. And now her older sister came to her with an idea. The tragedy of this whole thing is that it's pretty obvious that the older sister didn't learn this kind of behavior from her dad. When Abram and Lot decided to go their separate ways, Abram gave Lot the choice of the direction and land he wanted to go. Unfortunately for Lot, the place he chose had a deceivingly pleasant outward appearance. The place he chose to live was full of sin, more specifically sexual sin. There's no evidence that Lot was in any way corrupted. Actually, in 2 Peter, we read that Lot stayed righteous, and it actually was very distressing to Lot having to live among such wickedness. Second Peter 2:7–8 reads,

> And delivered just Lot, vexed with the filthy conversation of the wicked: (for that righteous man dwelling among them, in seeing and hearing, vexed his righteous soul from day to day with their unlawful deeds).

So what I'm saying is this: even though it appears that Lot wasn't corrupted by living among such wickedness, his daughter learned her evil ways from someone, someone she didn't choose to live around. Think about public schools. Somewhere kids are almost forced to go. Kids aren't exactly excited about going to school. They don't choose to go; it's something that the world has just decided is the way of life. Parents send their children to school. Sometimes it's parents who went to school themselves without being corrupted, which causes them to never feel a need to properly prepare their children for the upcoming struggles they may face. But where do most kids begin learning their rebellious ways? That's right—somewhere along the lines of school, school-related activity, or an event that was planned with classmates from school. The younger daughter seems to be a victim of peer pressure here. It wasn't her idea, but being told to do it and seeing her sister do it, she followed in her sister's very sinful act.

If we heard on the news today that two daughters got their father drunk and had sex with him and are now both carrying children by their father, it would be one of the hottest topics in the world. People would describe it as sickening and talk about it in a voice that displays excitement. People would be searching the Internet to read about this headline. How many people even know about this story in the Bible?

It's Easier to Follow

Wouldn't it be great if we all had the strength and integrity to not follow in what we know is wrong? Joseph was a young man with big dreams, which caused jealousy that led to very evil intentions. Genesis 37:19 reads,

> And they said to one another, Behold, this dreamer cometh. Come now therefore, and let us slay him, and cast him into some pit, and we will say, Some evil beast hath devoured him: and we will see what will become of his dreams.

Now, if you're not familiar with this story and you didn't take the time to read what led up to that point, I'll try to, as briefly and accurately as possible, bring you up to speed on what happened. The dreamer who they are speaking of is Joseph. Jacob had many sons, but he loved Joseph the most because he was the son born to him in his old age. It was very obvious that Joseph was loved more as his father gave him a special coat, and Joseph was strongly disliked, or even hated, by his brothers. Then to add insult to injury, Joseph had dreams of greatness. This did not sit well Joseph's brothers, so much that they secretly plotted to kill him. Now that I've brought you up to speed, let's look at the oldest brother's response. Genesis 37:21 reads,

> And Reuben heard it, and he delivered him out of their hands; and said, Let us not kill him. And Reuben said unto them, Shed no blood, but cast him into this pit that is in the wilderness, and lay no hand upon him; that he might rid him out of their hands, to deliver him to his father again.

Now, I can only wonder if being the oldest in the family, Reuben could have gotten his brothers to see that what they were doing was wrong and convinced them to do away with their evil plot altogether, but that's neither here nor there, considering the words of Joseph in Genesis 45:5:

> Now therefore be not grieved, nor angry with yourselves, that ye sold me hither: for God did send me before you to preserve life.

The point I'm trying to make is, sometimes, just as easy as it is to convince someone to join in evil, the same could be said about convincing someone to join in doing the right thing. If you're familiar with the rest of this story, we see that because Reuben only planned to do his good deed in secret, he never got the chance to do so, for his brothers had other plans. Verse 23 picks up with Joseph arriving at the place his brothers were, and they stripped him from the coat his father had given him, and they cast him into a pit, which was going according to Reuben's plan as he would then have the opportunity to save his brother secretly. The only problem was, another brother had other plans. Listen to Genesis 37:26:

> And Judah said unto his brethren, What profit is it if we slay our brother, and conceal his blood? Come, and let us sell him to the Ishmeelites, and let not our hand be upon him; for his is our brother and our flesh. And his brethren were content.

Notice that at one point, they had a plan, a plan to kill their brother out of jealousy. Two of Joseph's brothers each had different plans. One came forward with his plan; the other tried to do it in secret. The brother who came forward with his idea was, without dispute, able to get his brothers to agree to a change in plan. It seems to me this world is full of followers. Everyone likes to be part of something that's going on, but who is willing to stand up for what is right? Who is willing to stand up and say, "I will not follow in evil," or at least just refuse to follow in evil? I can name one man who showed his loyalty to a friend, as well as displaying his integrity and ability to be his own man, not caring who or what was telling him be a follower of sin. Have you ever heard of a young man who goes by the name Jonathan? Not exactly known for slaying giants or rebuilding walls that had lain in ruins for decades. He wasn't one of Jesus's disciples. He didn't help lead the Israelites out of Egypt. He was simply a king's son and a future king's best friend. Jonathan was a man whom

I admire more and more every time I read about him. We read earlier how easy it was for a mother to convince her son to do what he knew was wrong and could earn him a punishment. Let me remind you of a young man who was so obedient to his father that he followed him right to what was going to be his deathbed.

Whom Do You Trust?

I'm sure you're all familiar with the story of Abraham's test of faith as he was to offer his long-awaited son Isaac. Poor Isaac followed his father without question all the way to what could have been his end. But the man I want to focus on right now is a man who violated commandment number five in what I can only describe as an incredible act of integrity. First Samuel 19 begins with,

> And Saul spake to Jonathan his son, and to all his servants, that they should kill David. But Jonathan Saul's son delighted much n David: and Jonathan told David, saying, Saul my father seeketh to kill thee: now therefore, I pray thee, take heed to thyself until the morning, and abide in a secret place, and hide thyself: and I will go out and stand beside my father in the field where thou art, and I will commune with my father of thee and what I see, that I will tell thee.

Now, had David done something wrong, I could see Jonathan being the type of man who may stand up for what is right and possibly try to kill David himself. But if you know the story, you know that Saul gave David a job to do; and after David did it so well that it took away from Saul's glory, Saul grew jealous of David. First Samuel 18:5–9 reads,

> And David went out whithersoever Saul sent him, and behaved himself wisely: and Saul set him over the men of war, and he was accepted in the sight of all the people, and also in the sight of Saul's servants. And it came to pass as they came, when David was returned from the slaughter of the Philistine, that the women came out of all the cities of Israel, singing and dancing, to meet king Saul with tabrets, joy, and with instruments of musick. And the women answered one another as they played, and said, Saul hath slain his thousands and David his ten thousands. And Saul was very wroth, and the saying displeased him; and he said, They have ascribed unto David ten thousands, and to me they have ascribed but thousands: and what can he have more but the kingdom? And Saul eyed David from that day and forward.

From this point on, Jonathan went through great lengths to defy his father's wishes and keep David safe. Can you imagine how different the world would be if it had more Jonathans? Humans who would not follow in sin no matter who it is that is telling them. Humans full of integrity and not insecurity, which leads them to being victimized by the treacherous thing called peer pressure. Unfortunately, it's not always that easy. Saul never expected his own son to be what stopped him from killing his enemy.

But let's now look at an instance where persistence paid off in what I call another act of following in sin. Judges chapter 14:12

begins with Samson proclaiming a riddle. He says that he will give thirty changes of clothing to anyone who can give the answer to his riddle within seven days. Judges 14:16–17 reads,

> And Samon's wife wept before him, and said, Thou dost but hate me, and lovest me not: thou has put forth a riddle unto the children of my people, and hast not told it me. And he said unto her, behold, I have not told it my father nor my mother, and shall I tell it thee? And she wept before him the seven days, while their feast lasted: and it came to pass on the seventh day, that he told her, because she lay sore upon him: and she told the riddle to the children of her people.

So why did Samson's wife care so much about the answer to this riddle? Well, if you have read the story for yourself, or at least verse 15, you'd know that she was following—I repeat, *following*—orders. Judges 14:15 reads,

> And it came it pass on the seventh day, that they said unto Samson's wife, Entice thy husband, that he may declare unto us the riddle, lest we burn thee and thy father's house with fire.

Listen to Samson's response:

> And he said unto them, If ye had not plowed with my heifer, ye had not found out my riddle.

Samson never expected anyone to solve his riddle, and when he told his wife the answer, he never suspected she would give his answer to the enemy. This angered Samson to the point that he then went and killed thirty men and took their clothes and gave them to the men who answered his riddle. Now let's continue on with Samson's story. He managed to once again find him a woman who would follow the orders of others. Judges 16: 4 reads,

> And it came to pass afterward, that the loved a woman in the valley of Sorek, whose name was Delilah. And the lords of the Philistines came up unto her, and said unto her, Entice him, and see wherein his great strength lieth, and by what means we may prevail against him that we ma bind him to afflict him: and we will give thee every one of us eleven hundred pieces of silver.

So what was Delilah following? Well, yes, she was following orders, but more specifically, she was following the love of money. Now we will take a look at the persistence of Delilah to get Samson to do what he did not want to do. In Judges 16:6, 10, and 13, Samson, not wanting to give out the secret to where his strength lay, lied to Delilah. This only caused Delilah to use a manipulation tactic that many humans have fallen victim to. Judges 16:15 reads,

> And she said unto him, How canst thou say, I love thee, when thine heart is not with me? Thou has mocked me these three times, and hast not told me where in thy great strength lieth.

In verse 16, Samson finally gave in and did what he very obviously did not want to do. He told her where his strength lay, which eventually led to his death, but only after tremendous suffering. If being deceived by his own wife wasn't bad enough, what came next had to be all a man should ever have to endure. Judges 16:21 reads,

> But the Philistines took him, and put out his eyes, and brought him down to Gaza, and bound him with fetters of brass; and he did grind in the prison house.

Now, those are some pretty harsh repercussions for revealing your own secret. It's no wonder he didn't want to tell it sooner. Can you remember a time when someone asked you to do something you didn't want to do but the persistent peer pressure finally broke you and you gave in and, as a result, some unfortunate event took place afterward? I remember in junior high school, a few of my friends had begun smoking cigarettes. One friend in particular was very persistent in asking me to smoke; finally, I gave in. One day, my mom smelled the smoke on me, and I was caught. I had said no many times, but finally I gave in for no apparent reason other than just to get my friend to stop asking. Most of us can't relate to having a secret of superhuman strength revealed and it leading to torture, but if we substitute a few words, we can all relate to these examples of people following in sin. First John 5:17 describes sin as "all wrongdoing" (ESV). I think more people can relate to the ways of the younger daughter of Lot and of Samson, who followed sin, rather than of Jonathan, who went against his father's wishes to do what was right. But the unfortunate truth about all these examples is that most of us are more like Reuben, who had the thought to do right, but because we didn't come forward with our true feelings, we had to watch sin right before our very eyes. James 4:17 says that just to know what the right thing to do and not do it is sin. With all that said, we now must look to why we get so caught up in following sin. Well, it's usually not really that we are following sin but the sinner. We are watching someone who is what I call a *leader* in sin.

Chapter 5

LEADERS IN SIN

In the previous chapter, we briefly went over how Lot's two daughters got their father drunk to have sex with him, something that is very wrong. So we don't exactly know where the older daughter got these kinds of evil thoughts; all we know is that she got the idea from somewhere, and now she had become a leader in sin, leading her younger sister to join in her sinful act. So now let's take a look at how exactly she went about doing such a thing. The best definition of a leader I've ever heard is something along the lines of "getting someone to do what they wouldn't normally do, and do it without complaining." So how did the older sister go about doing that? First of all, she used a five-step process for which I have no specific name: (1) she justified it, (2) she planned it, (3) she removed the obstacles, (4) she did it herself, (5) she reminded her sister why they were doing it and that it was now her turn. Let's look at each of these five acts:

Step 1. "And the firstborn said unto the younger, Our father is old, and there is not a man in the earth to come in unto us after the manner of all the earth" (Genesis 19:31). Wasn't that nice of her? Lot's daughter was very concerned for her father, realizing that there was no one to carry out his family name. This was something that Abraham was so concerned about, that, while very rich, he told God that it was all meaningless. If you take away all the evil and sickness that was done to achieve this goal, it actually was a very thoughtful thing.

Step 2. "We will lie with him, that we may preserve seed of our father" (Genesis 19:32). Have you heard of the term *improvise*? That's exactly what she did. Since her and her sister's husbands were no longer around, nor was their mother, they did it as the only way that was actually possible at that very moment.

Step 3. "Come, let us make our father drink wine" (Genesis 19:32). Well, at this point, it's safe to say that Lot's oldest daughter knew that her father wouldn't go for such an act as she used alcohol to take away Lot's ability to function to the point that both daughters were able to do the deed without him ever knowing. The last words of verse 33 and 35 both read, "And he perceived not when she lay down, nor when she arose."

Step 4. "And the firstborn went in, and lay with her father" (Genesis 19:33). How often is it that when someone tells us to do something we haven't done, we can easily think something along the lines of, *Why are they telling me to do it? Why don't they do it themselves?* This could be something as simple as trying a new food a family member cooked. Once you see that someone else has done it, all reluctance is gone. You think, *Well, they did it. I guess I can do it too.* This is probably the most important step of the five, or at least the most convincing. Lots of people plan things that never get done, usually because they aren't willing to do it themselves or simply don't want to do it alone.

Step 5. "And it came to pass on the morrow, that the firstborn said unto the younger, Behold, I lay yesternight with my father: let us make him drink wine this night also; and go thou in, and lie with him, that we may preserve seed of our father...and the younger arose, and lay with him" (Genesis 19:34–35). So after Lot's oldest daughter went in and lay with her father, which meant that they had already done what they set out to do, that wasn't good enough. She didn't want to do it alone. She now turned to her sister and basically said, "See? I did it. Now you do it too."

So to sum up what I just tried to teach you, let me simply put it like this: up to a certain point in our lives, everything we do is because we learned it—from someone, somehow, someway. Then at some point, we no longer need to be shown how to do it. We know how to do it, and we can then do it ourselves. We then take the chance of becoming a leader. Only problem is, we don't know who is going to be following. When Moses killed the Egyptian, he looked around first and then buried the body, thinking his secret was safe. The next day, it was revealed that he, in fact, had been seen. In Genesis 26:8, Isaac was watched through a window when he thought he was doing it in private. These are simply times when someone is being watched without them knowing it, but that's the first step to unknowingly becoming a leader in sin.

I gave you a definition of the word *leader* earlier; now I'm going to give you another. A leader can simply be someone who doesn't have to be a follower to do something. Let us now look to a couple of men who led themselves straight to sin. So to begin, I guess let's start with the first murder in the Bible. Up to that point, no man had ever committed murder, so where did he learn it? Well, we don't know that, but we do know that many people followed in his sinful act. In Genesis chapter 4, Cain killed his own brother out of jealousy. Cain and Abel had been given duties. Abel was a keeper of sheep, but Cain was a tiller of the ground. Genesis 4:3–5 reads,

> And in process of time it came to pass, that Cain brought of the fruit of the ground an offering unto the Lord. And Abel, he also brought of the firstlings of his flock and of the fat thereof. And the Lord had respect unto Abel and to his

offering: but unto Cain and to his offering he had no respect. And Cain was very wroth, and his countenance fell.

After this, God asked Cain why he was so angry and made this statement in verse 7:

If thou doest well, shalt thou not be accepted? And if thou doest not well, sin lieth at the door. And unto thee shall be his desire, and thou shalt rule over him.

In the very next verse, Cain was doing something he'd never seen before, something he was not simply following in. Genesis 4:8 reads,

And Cain talked with Abel his brother: and it came to pass, when they were in the field, that Cain rose up against Abel is brother and slew him.

Now, if that wasn't bad enough, Cain did something else I see no evidence he'd ever seen done before. He lied to God and did it in an insolent manner. When Adam was asked by God if he did something wrong, Adam didn't try to lie about it, so we can't say he was following in his father's footsteps. Genesis 4:9 reads,

And the Lord said unto Cain, Where is Abel thy brother? And he said, I know not: Am I my brother's keeper?

God immediately let Cain know that he couldn't lie to him and asked him what he had done. Genesis 4:10 reads,

> And he said, What hast thou done? The voice of thy brother's blood crieth unto me from the ground.

Led into Sin

We've now discussed a couple of humans who either led someone else into following them in a sin or simply creating a new sin without having to follow someone else. Remember how Lot's oldest daughter justified her sin by at least saying they were doing something good for their father? Well, here is a very unfortunate situation. Moses was chosen to lead the Israelites out of their slavery in Egypt, but because he didn't think he was up to the task, God sort of appointed him a partner, but that never changed the fact that Moses was the chosen leader. We are about to see why God wanted Moses, and only Moses, to be the leader.

Exodus chapter 32 begins with Moses still being in the presence of God just after receiving the Ten Commandments. He'd been away from the Israelites for forty days, and the Israelites began to question why they were out wandering in the wilderness without a leader. Exodus 32:1 reads,

> And when the people saw that Moses delayed to come down out of the mount, the people gathered themselves together unto Aaron, and said unto him, Up, make us gods which shall go before us; for as for this Moses, the man that

brought us up out of the land of Egypt, we wot not what is become of him.

Aaron, not really being a true leader, not knowing how to handle the situation, told them to take off all their gold jewelry, and he would make them something to worship. Exodus 32:4 reads,

> And he received them at their hand and fashioned it with a graving tool, after he had made it a molten calf: and they said, These be thy gods, O Israel, which brought thee up out of the land of Egypt.

So what Aaron did, possibly not even knowing exactly what he was doing, just led the Israelites right into sin, a sin so bad that it almost cost them their lives had it not been for their real leader Moses leading them back on the right path. Exodus 32:10 reads,

> Now therefore let me alone, that my wrath may wax hot against them, and that I may consume them: and I will make of thee a great nation.

There are many definitions of what a leader is exactly. But one of the qualities that should be in a true leader is that you have to be able to trust them. Now, obviously, the Israelites trusted Aaron, but the problem was that they shouldn't have. But before I put Aaron down, let's remember that Moses was the one chosen to be their leader, not Aaron. He wasn't ready to be their leader; he basically just wanted to keep the thousands of complaining humans happy because he simply didn't know how to handle them. Luckily for them, their true leader knew how to handle the situation properly as he pleaded to God for their sakes and reminded him of his promise to Abraham.

Aaron then led himself right into another sin, proving why God didn't just choose him in the first place. Exodus 32:23–24 reads,

> For they said unto me, Make us gods, which shall go before us: for as for this Moses, the man that brought us up out of the land of Egypt, we wot not what is become of him. And I said unto them, Whosoever hath any gold, let them break it off. So they gave it to me: then I cast it into the fire, and there came out this calf.

So Aaron, proving he should have never been in charge as he was explaining himself to the true leader, told mostly the truth. But then he finished it off with a bold-faced lie as he said he simply put the gold in the fire, and a golden calf came out. I guess he didn't count on there being so many witnesses, for if it wasn't God himself who told Moses what really happened, which is very possible, it was surely one of the Israelites who were watching. If you didn't already know, Moses wrote the book of Exodus himself, and he wasn't there when Aaron made this calf, which we clearly saw in verse 4 was made with his own hand—"and fashioned it with a graving tool."

As a result of this, three thousand Israelites were killed by their own people. God had to find out who were serious about turning from other gods, so he had Moses ask the people whoever was on the Lord's side to come to him, and then God had them go out and kill the ones who weren't. Exodus 32:26–27 reads,

> Then Moses stood in the gate of the camp, and said, Who is on the Lord's side? Let him come unto me. And all the sons of Levi gathered themselves together unto him. And he said unto them, Thus saith the Lord God of Israel,

> Put every man his sword by his side, and go in and out from gate to gate throughout the camp, and slay every man his brother, and every man his companion, and every man his neighbor.

Another man who needed no one right in front of him to show him his sin was David. Earlier, we discussed David's sin involving adultery, deceit, murder, and a number of broken commandments. When we're no longer following anyone—meaning, as long as we do what we are told, we think we are doing the right thing—we then have a chance to realize something. If we are putting effort into our sins, we've done something nobody wants to do. We've arrived at the *wrong destination*.

CHAPTER 6

THE WRONG DESTINATION

I remember a time I was headed home from a friend's house who lived out in the country. I got in my truck and started driving just as I had done many times before. I was just driving along the highway as usual, taking a route that was only supposed to be a ten- to fifteen-mile drive if you go the right way. I was so lost in thought and never thought to look at the time that I had no idea I was going the wrong way until I saw unfamiliar scenery. I immediately called my sister and described to her what I was seeing. She proceeded to tell me I was in a town that was closer to forty-five miles away. How I turned a fifteen-minute trip into an almost-two-hour trip after it was all said and done is beyond me. I had been heading in the wrong direction for close to forty-five minutes, but I never cared until I knew without a doubt that I was arriving at the wrong destination.

Remember how David reacted when it was brought to his attention that what he was doing was wrong. David was so caught up in his sin that he was constantly working on a new plan to cover his sin, thus moving further and further from the man he once was. In 2 Samuel 11:2, David spotted what would turn into sin, and by verse

4, he was fully engaged in sin. It wasn't until chapter 12:13 that he realized he was at the wrong destination. Second Samuel 12:13 reads,

> And David said unto Nathan, I have sinned against the Lord.

If you read from 2 Samuel 11:2–12:13, you'll see that the entire time, David was headed in the wrong direction. Without consequences, it's sometimes hard to realize that what you're doing is wrong because you're doing what you want to do. In my situation, I was doing exactly what I wanted to do. I was driving up to the point I realized that I wasn't where I wanted to be, but I still had no idea where I was until my sister told me. David never stopped to think about where he was until God sent Nathan to inform him.

Destination: Guilt and Fear

David and I aren't the only humans who have found ourselves at the wrong destination in life. Here are a few more men of the Bible who, at some point, realized they were, in fact, at the wrong destination. Genesis 42:21–22 reads,

> And they said to one another, We are verily guilty concerning our brother in that we saw the anguish of his soul when he besought us, and we would not hear; therefore is this distress come upon us. And Reuben answered, saying, Spake I not unto you, saying, Do not sin against the child; and ye would not hear.

It had been over a decade since they had set off in the wrong direction in life as they plotted to kill their brother and had him sold into slavery. But they never seemed to care until things got tough. The land had been overtaken by famine, and they were now traveling to Egypt to get food for survival. What they didn't know was that the only man who could help them was the very man whom they'd sold and never cared to see again. Now they were in quite the predicament. Joseph knew who they were and was actually kind of playing a game with them. He told them they must bring their younger brother to him. This wasn't exactly a simple task, considering their father refused to let it happen. They were now, for the first time, in a very tough situation, and the guilt began to set in. They had no proof that their sinful act was the reason they were now close to suffering, but that was all they could think of as to why this was happening. At that moment, they finally regretted what they'd done and realized that they were at the wrong destination. Had they just been able to go buy their grain and return home, it just would have been life. But because of everything they'd done, it wasn't that simple. When I finally realized that I was completely in the wrong city, I was now almost triple the distance away from my destination as when I started. Joseph's brothers had to make multiple trips back and forth, bargaining with their father, Joseph, and simply buying grain.

In chapter 43:10, Judah was getting so frustrated with the situation that he told his father that they were now just wasting time. Sometimes realizing you're at the wrong destination isn't something you can do on your own. For instance, if you have never seen the destination you are heading to, you wouldn't know that you arrived at the wrong destination, unless you arrived somewhere else you had already been and were familiar with because you then would certainly know you hadn't planned to arrive there again, or at least not at that moment.

The Forced Correction

Now to make my point, I see no other way than to include a story in which a man had arrived at a destination so bad that Jesus Christ himself had to perform a miracle to get this man headed in the right direction. Acts 9:1–9 reads,

> And Saul, yet breathing out threatenings and slaughter against the disciples of the Lord, went unto the high priest, and desired of him letters to Damascus to the synagogues, that if he found any of his way, whether they were men or women, he might bring them bound unto Jerusalem. And as he journeyed, he came near Damascus: and suddenly there shined round about him a light from heaven: and he fell to the earth, and heard a voice saying unto him, Saul, Saul, why persecutes thou me? And he said, Who art thou, Lord? And the Lord Said, I am Jesus whom thou persecutes: it is hard for thee to kick against the pricks. And he trembling and astonished said, Lord, what wilt thou have me to do? And the Lord said unto him, Arise, and go into the city, and it shall be told thee what thou must do. And the men which journeyed with him stood speechless, hearing a voice, but seeing no man. And Saul arose from the earth; and when his eyes were opened, he saw no man: but they led him by the hand, and brought him into Damascus. And he was three days without sight, and neither die eat or drink.

Now, for you non-Bible scholars, I'll bring you up to speed a little bit. Saul is more widely known as Paul, the same Paul who wrote the books Romans, 1 and 2 Corinthians, Galatians, Ephesians, Philippians, Colossians, 1 and 2 Thessalonians, 1 and 2 Timothy, Titus, Philemon, and Hebrews. This man was not always the Jesus lover he became, the man who loved Jesus to the point he, in Philippians 1:23, said that he was ready to die and go be with Jesus. But while Paul was still known as Saul, he was as far from the man who was writing those books as it gets. Paul was widely known for persecuting Christians. Acts chapter 6 begins with the twelve apostles appointing men to help care for the widows in their ministry. They chose seven men, one being Stephen, described as "a man full of faith and of the Holy Ghost." This man stood up and proclaimed the Word of God, and for his actions, he was stoned. Acts 7:57–60 reads,

> Then they cried out with a loud voice, and stopped their ears, and ran upon him with one accord, and cast him out of the city, and stoned him: and the witnesses laid down their clothes at a young man's feet whose name was Saul. And they stoned Stephen, calling upon God, and saying, Lord Jesus, receive my spirit. And he kneeled down, and cried with a loud voice, Lord, lay not this sin to their charge. And when he had said this, he fell asleep.

How did Paul feel about this? Acts 8:1–3 reads,

> And Saul was consenting unto his death. And devout men carried Stephen to his burial, and made great lamentation over him. As for Saul, he made havock of the church, entering into

every house, and hailing men and women committed them to prison.

I want to share one more important verse before I finish making the point I'm trying to make right now. Acts 9:15 reads, "But the Lord said unto him, Go thy way: for he is a chosen vessel unto me, to bear my name before the Gentiles, and kings, and the children of Israel." Now, the man whom he was speaking to in that verse was a man known as "a certain disciple." Ananias was spoken to by the Lord in a vision, telling him to go and find Saul. Ananias was not that happy about the words spoken to him, for verse 9:13 reads, "Then Ananias answered, Lord, I have heard by many of this man, how much evil he hath done to thy saints at Jerusalem." The destination that Saul had arrived at was so bad, so wrong, that everyone knew where he had been. Just as he is widely known in today's world for the great things he did in Jesus's name, the days this was all happening, he was more widely known for the opposite.

So far in this book, the main focus has been set on the mistakes of humans of the past. I didn't even have to include stories such as Sarah giving her maid to her husband, Abraham, with the bright idea to give him a son, which only lead to her jealousy to the point she sent a young boy and his mother—who did nothing but follow her orders and carry out the plan that Sarah herself concocted—out of their home with nowhere to go. If you're unfamiliar with this, read about it yourself in Genesis chapter 16.

From the beginning of time, humans have been doing things that they later regret, but the most unfortunate sin is a sin that comes from what we originally thought were good intentions. Those are the times that lead me to truly understand exactly how good humans are at making mistakes. Now I believe it's time to begin looking at how to start correcting these mistakes. When I found out I was at the wrong destination in my small journey, to turn a fifteen-minute trip into a two-hour trip, I immediately changed the direction I was heading. Now, that doesn't mean I was immediately at the right destination. It took time, and now I was paying extra attention to everything I was doing. And I did, in fact, end up at the right destination. All the stories that we've previously reviewed, none of them really have the part where they realized they were in the wrong and then did something to correct their mistakes. Once you've realized that you have arrived at the wrong destination, before you arrive at the right direction, there's one thing you have to do first: you must change the direction in which you were headed.

PART 2

The Present (Where You Are)

The purpose of a compass is not just to give us knowledge about where we are when we are lost but to also guide us into the way we need to go.

It feels like angels and demons are playing a game of tug-of-war with my soul.

CHAPTER 7

CHANGING DIRECTION (REPENTANCE)

Before you can rightfully change direction, you have to admit that you were, or are, headed in the wrong direction. So what does it take to make you realize that you are heading in the wrong direction?

Wouldn't it been nice if on the first wrong turn I made, I had realized that I was now heading in the wrong direction? I could have stopped, looked for cars, made an illegal U-turn, and been headed on my way. My ten- to fifteen-minute drive would have become an eleven- to sixteen-minute drive, and you wouldn't have had to read about it. My sister wouldn't have had to be bothered while she was at work, and I would have saved time, gas, money, and the embarrassment of not being able to find my way home without a trail of bread crumbs. Unfortunately, it's not always that easy. Here's another unfortunate truth to the matter: even when I had realized I was at the wrong place, had I not had my sister to guide me, I never would have even known which direction to head to. I know I'm not the only one in the world who has ever needed someone else to help tell me which direction to head to. Simon Peter was a man who was a sinning fisherman. Jesus decided it was time for Peter to change direction. Luke 5:4–8 reads,

> Now when he had left speaking, he said unto Simon, Launch out into the deep, and let down your nets for a draught. And Simon answering said unto him, Master, we have toiled all night, and have taken nothing: nevertheless at thy word I will let down the net. And when they had this done, they inclosed a great multitude of fishes: and their net brake. And they beckoned unto their partners, which were in the other ship, theat they shoud come and help them. And they came, and filled both ships, so that they began to sink. When Simon Peter saw it, he fell down at Jesus' knees, saying, Depart from me; for I am a sinful man, O Lord.

Now if you're familiar with this portion of the Bible, you'll know that Jesus's response to Simon Peter was, "Fear not; from henceforth thou shalt catch men," which was taken from verse 10. The following verse reads, "And when they had brought their ships to land, they forsook all, and followed him." Now, if you're reading Matthew, which seems to tell the same story, but just not in as much detail, chapter 4:18–19 reads,

> And Jesus, walking by the sea of Galilee, saw two brethren, Simon called Peter, and Andrew his brother, casting net into the sea: for they were fishers. And he saith unto them, Follow me, and I will make you fishers of men.

What I want you to take special note is what Jesus said to them, two things in particular, one being the words, "Follow me." If someone came up to you, whether you know them or not, and told you to come with them, you're probably going to ask them where they're going or simply why. The second is Jesus telling them why he wanted them to follow him. He basically told them they had arrived at the wrong destination in life. They were not supposed to be at a place where they were catching fish for a living. They would now fish for men. Now, just because you have changed direction after realizing that you had arrived at the wrong destination, that doesn't mean your path is now set, and you have an autopilot that will be taking over and you can just enjoy the road to your desired destination. As I stated earlier, after I had started heading in the right direction, I was constantly looking at signs; listening to my sister, who became my guide; and from that point on, riding home, which was supposed to be so simple that I felt no need to pay attention at all. What I had set out to do and had done so many times before had now become the most stressful ride of my life.

I was afraid to make a single decision on my own. I desperately wanted to get home and literally couldn't afford to make another mistake. From the time, Simon Peter was told by Jesus that he would now have to change direction and begin changing his life. Peter was willing to do what Jesus wanted, but that didn't make it easy. Peter began following Jesus, but not without mistakes.

Even after Peter had changed his direction, Jesus had to correct him on several occasions. Even though he wasn't willingly returning to his old ways, he was beginning to veer off into the wrong direction. Fortunately for Peter, he had Jesus right in front of him to correct him as he made his mistakes.

Just because you've changed direction doesn't mean you're heading in the right direction. My friend's home was located just outside of a small town directly east, about ten miles away from my home.

There had been times while driving at night that I missed my turn onto a dirt road, and I'd see the lights of the small town and know that I had gone too far. I'd turn around and may have wasted five minutes but then knew I was, without a doubt, on the right road. I was not at all familiar with the city I had ended up in, and it was about forty-five miles southeast of my home. Had I left that city without a guide, it's possible I could have gone in another direction, heading farther away without even knowing it. Had I just seen lights and turned around, I could have easily made it back to where I came from; but because I headed so far into the city before turning around, I was completely lost.

Now, instead of one right direction to go, I had many wrong directions to go. Peter suffered from what I just spoke of, heading in the wrong direction. Remember when Jesus's disciples saw him walking on water? Peter called out to Jesus and said, "Lord if it be thou, bid me come unto thee on the water." Peter obviously wanted to follow Jesus to the right destination. I mean, the man was willing to try what, up to this point in his life, was impossible. Peter was a fisherman. He had been out on the water countless of times, and never before did he have the ability to walk on water before. Why would this day be any different? It doesn't say Peter was filled with the Holy Ghost or felt some supernatural power enter him that made him believe that he could now do what he couldn't do yesterday.

Peter simply wanted to believe that when Jesus said follow him, he meant it. Why would Jesus say, "Follow me," then go somewhere that he knew nobody else could go? Peter stepped out onto the water but began to sink. The wind picked up, which scared Peter, and he no longer believed he could do what he was already doing. He cried to Jesus, "Lord, save me." He was headed in the right direction as he stepped out onto the water, but just as quick as he took a tremendous leap of faith, his direction changed. How did Jesus react to this? "And immediately Jesus stretched forth his hand, and caught him and said unto him, O thou of little faith, wherefore didst thou doubt?" Jesus immediately corrected Peter when he made a mistake. If you would like to read the entire story for yourself, you can read it in Matthew 14:22–33. I'm now going to provide a list of other times where Peter began heading in the wrong direction, but Jesus was there to quickly get him to change his direction again, ensuring he didn't end up too far off the path he was supposed to be on.

Matthew 16:21–23. After Jesus told his disciples he must go to Jerusalem and suffer, Peter thought he was doing the right thing and said, "Lord: this shall not be unto thee." Jesus quickly corrected Peter by saying, "Get thee behind me, Satan: thou art an offence unto me: for thou savourest not the things that be of God, but those of men."

Matthew 26:51–52. Peter drew his sword and cut off a man's ear, defending Jesus. Jesus responded to this by saying, "Put up again thy sword into his place: for all they that take the sword shall perish with the sword." Then he undid what Peter did as he healed the man's ear. If that wasn't showing someone that they were headed in the wrong direction, I don't know what is.

Matthew 26:69–75. This is a moment when Peter was in serious danger of once again arriving at the "wrong destination." This was when Peter denied ever knowing Jesus. Jesus was no longer around to correct Peter face-to-face, but he did give him a huge sign that he was headed in the wrong direction as he made sure he heard the crow, which then triggered Peter to remember the words Jesus had already spoken to him.

Later, I'll be using the life of Peter to show what can happen to someone who changes direction and then continues in the right direction, but the title of this chapter is "Changing Direction." Let's now recall a man who was first headed in the right direction but changed direction and was then more than prodded by God himself back in the right direction.

You Can't Run from God

Now, up to this point, Jonah was obviously doing something right as he was chosen by God to go preach to others. God told Jonah he was to go to Nineveh, but Jonah didn't like this plan at all. Jonah 1:3 reads,

> But Jonah rose up to flee unto Tarshish from the presence of the Lord, and went down to Joppa; and he found a ship going to Tarshish: so he paid the fare thereof, and went down into it, to go with them unto Tarshish from the presence of the Lord.

So Jonah, who was just headed in the right direction as he obviously had earned the respect and trust of God, now started heading so far in the wrong direction that God took matters into his own hands. Jonah 1:4 reads,

> But the Lord sent out a great wind into the sea, and there was a mighty tempest in the sea, so that the ship was like to be broken.

Now, you'd think that might have been enough to get Jonah headed back in the right direction, but it wasn't. Instead, he told the men to throw him overboard as he'd rather die than change direction. God wasn't about to let that happen. Jonah was swallowed by a great fish (Jonah 1:17), where he stayed in what I could hardly call a five-star hotel for three days and three nights until finally he prayed to God. Jonah 2:10 reads,

> And the Lord spake unto the fish, and it vomited out Jonah upon the dry land.

So as I mentioned earlier, sometimes we never know that we need to change directions until we've already arrived at the wrong destination. Unfortunately, we don't always have Jesus right next to us to point out when we do something wrong. The next thing we have to consider is, once we change direction, what direction are we going to head to? Sometimes heading in the wrong direction after arriving at the wrong destination can only lead us further from our target location. So that brings me to this very important question that someone who is lost may ask, Where do we go from there?

A map tells you where you've been, where you are, and where you are going to be!

Chapter 8

Where to Go from There (Born Again)

I do not know the path he leads me, but well do I know my guide.

The unfortunate truth in the answer to the closing question of my last chapter is, most of us have no idea what it is that God is telling us to do. I read the quote posted above approximately ten years ago. It became one of my favorite quotes, and it truly meant a lot to me. I used it for inspiration and tried to find a way to use it for motivation. It wasn't until about a year ago that I finally figured out the true meaning of it.

When I claimed this as one of my favorite quotes and used it like it made perfect sense for my life, I was still missing a huge part of it. Fact is, I knew almost nothing about my "guide." Once I began reading the Bible for myself and finally started understanding my "guide," the path he was leading me became very clear. You may think this next statement a little odd, considering what we just read about Jonah, but here it goes: we aren't all as fortunate as Jonah! The last thing we read about Jonah, he was spat onto a beach by the great fish that swallowed him. Let's now continue reading chapter 3:

> And the word of the Lord came unto Jonah the second time, saying, Arise, go unto Nineveh, that great city, and preach unto it the preaching that I bid thee. So Jonah arose, and went unto Nineveh, according to the word of the Lord.

See, Jonah knew exactly what he was supposed to do; and after putting up a bit of a fight, changing directions, ending up at the wrong destination(who wants to be in the belly of a fish?), he once again changed direction and did what God had already told him to do. I'm hoping if you don't know what God is telling you to do or "where to go from there," the rest of this book will help you realize you've known longer than you think; you just didn't know it. Whether you know it or not, simply realizing you were headed the wrong way or ended up at the wrong place is a tremendous step toward arriving at the correct and ultimate destination.

Becoming a Follower—of Jesus

You must now realize you are no longer a "leader" you first had to follow to learn how to sin on your own and go your own way. Now you must once again become a follower, but this time, don't follow sin. Follow Jesus. Throughout the four Gospels, Jesus himself uses these two life-changing words, "Follow me." We see it for the first time in Matthew 4:19. I want to make something very clear. Just because you know where to go doesn't mean you are going to get there without trouble or obstacles, and I'm certainly not saying you shouldn't make mistakes. These are some words I find very important in Christian living, written by Paul in his letter to the Philippians, verse 3:13: "Brethren, I count not myself to have apprehended: but this one thing I do, forgetting those things which are behind, and reaching forth unto those things which are before, press toward the mark for the prize of the high calling of God in Christ Jesus."

    Nobody on this earth is perfect, so it's safe to say that if you're reading this, you too are not perfect. Part of being a Christian is making the same mistakes you made before you were a Christian but viewing them in a different light. Some might claim they've always been a Christian, which may be very much true, so for those who fall into that category, let me give another line: part of being a Christian is realizing when you make a mistake without needing to be informed by the man next to you. The title of this chapter is "Where to Go from There," not "Now That You're Here." I'm now going to give you a small list of things I pulled from the first nine chapters of Luke. Jesus was so widely known for his miracles of turning water into wine, walking on water, feeding thousands of men and women with very little food. These are all things that nobody reading this should be able to do. I believe things like this are actually what cause our failure to realize that we have the ability to be more like Jesus than we think. I'm going to provide the verse and what I feel Jesus did that I believe anyone reading this can also do. If you read the story that the verse is taken from, you may think to yourself that you'll never even be in the position to do what Jesus did; but if you remove the story and look more closely at what exactly Jesus did, which you can also do, you'll find Jesus wasn't here to impress people with his miracles. Jesus was here to show us how to live. Here is a list of things that Jesus did that I feel anyone on this earth can do.

- Luke 4:16: Jesus stands up and reads out of the book of Isaiah.

- Luke 4:40: Jesus heals anyone who came to be healed (he turned away no one who wanted help).
- Luke 4:43: Jesus went out of his way to find people to help.
- Luke 5:4: Jesus helps others to do what they'd been trying to do but failed.
- Luke 5:10: Jesus begins to teach others to do as he does.
- Luke 5:16: Jesus often goes off to pray.
- Luke 6:10: Jesus takes no days off from doing what is right.
- Luke 6:27: Jesus helps someone who could easily be called his "enemy."
- Luke 9:13: Jesus doesn't send someone in need to find help elsewhere.
- Luke 9:28: Jesus takes others to pray.

Now to add to that list are a few of his most simple teachings:

- Luke 6:31: Do unto others as you want done unto you.
- Luke 6:33: Be the first to start the kindness cycle.
- Luke 6:34–35: Don't expect back in return.
- Luke 6:39: The blind can't lead the blind.
- Luke 6:41: Look at your faults before pointing out others'.
- Luke 9:5: Keep going; someone will appreciate you.

None of these are miraculous things. I'm now going to point out something that is very important to realize. This is actually one of the most unfortunate truths in becoming a true Christian. Luke 9:57–62 reads,

> And it came to pass, that, as they went in the way a certain man said unto him, Lord, I will follow thee whithersoever thou goest. And Jesus

> said unto him, Foxes have holes and birds of the air have nests; but the Son of man hath not where to lay his head. And he said unto another, Follow me. But he said, Lord, suffer me first to go and bury my father. Jesus said unto him, Let the dead bury their dead: but go thou and preach the kingdom of God. And another also said, Lord, I will follow thee; but let me first go bid them farewell, which are at home at my house. And Jesus said unto him, No man, having put his hand to the plough and looking back, is fit for the kingdom of God.

Did Jesus say that nothing is as important as following him? Not burying the dead, which is something we should have all been taught since we were young (that when someone dies, you attend the funeral even if it means taking off work or missing school). You mean Jesus is saying that you don't even have time to go say goodbye to your family? Well, let me bring to your attention a small story from the second chapter of Luke. Jesus and his family had gone to the Passover feast in Jerusalem, and afterward, when his family was heading back home, he stayed back without saying a single word to his family about what he was doing. He went to the temple to learn. Luke 2:48–50 says,

> And when they say him, they were amazed: and his mother said unto him, Son, why hast thou thus dealt with us? Behold, thy father and I have sought thee sorrowing. And he said unto them, How is it that ye sought me? Wist ye not that I must be about my Father's business? And they

understood not the saying which he spake unto them.

Jesus's parents didn't understand why their son would just leave his family without saying a word. I hope you now realize that Jesus simply demonstrated what he was telling others to do.

Although it's not exactly wrong to think that Jesus wants us to put following him above anything, even something like a funeral, that's not even what he meant in that scripture. The "dead" he was speaking about that he expected to do the burying were still very much alive, as far as still breathing or having a pulse and a heartbeat. What he was referring to was those who are spiritually dead.

Start Trusting in God, Jesus, and Yourself

I've now made a few of the points I hoped to make during this chapter, but now it's time to be a little more specific. What I'm trying to get at in this chapter is, start reading the Bible for yourself. Remember, I said that part of being a Christian is realizing your mistakes on your own. Well, that means you must know the scriptures.

I've begun to train my mind in the manner that if I see or hear something and it resembles something I've read in the Bible, I try to recall where it is in the Bible and how it pertains to the current situation. For example, one thing that is near impossible to make it through one single day without hearing or doing yourself is—complaining. Any time I hear someone complaining, or if I come to a point where I might possibly have to do something I don't want to do, I uncontrollably think of Philippians 2:14: "Do all things without murmurings and disputing." Honestly, there are times I wish I could forget that verse. I'm human, which means there are things I don't want to do; but if I can't create a reasonable argument or complaint about why not to do it, I can't justify not doing it.

How many times a day do you walk by a piece of trash that you don't pick up simply because you know you aren't the one who put it there? Don't you think that if God wanted it there, he would have made it himself? He made stars, humans, animals, etc. What was stopping him from making beer cans and Snickers wrappers if he wanted them all over the earth? Nowhere in the Bible does it say that if you see someone else's litter on the ground and walk by it without picking it up, you're doing something wrong. What I'm noticing, though, is that the more I read the Bible, the more I lose the ability to just ignore what is right.

I've mentioned that the key to figuring out where your next move should be from simply changing direction. I now want to point out the very unfortunate truth that prevents more people from just doing it. In Acts 8:26, the angel of the Lord spoke to Philip and told him to go meet a man who was riding on a chariot. The man was reading the book of Isaiah but took special note of verse 30.

> And Philip ran thither to him, and heard him read the prophet Esaias, and said, Understandest thou what thou readest? And he said, How can I, except some man should guide me? And he desired Philip that he would come up and sit with him.

There are actually two very unfortunate truths in this, one being that if you read the Bible as it is, it can be very hard to understand. Actually, it's so hard that it is disputed by Bible scholars everywhere. Nobody can prove that the way they have interpreted the Bible is absolutely correct, and simply because so many still dispute it. The second unfortunate truth is, even if someone is willing to read the

Bible, not everyone has someone to help them understand it. Most likely, if you read the Bible without actually getting anything from it, you're not going to continue to do it. The same thing could be said for many other things.

If you started a new diet that promised you so many pounds lost in so many days, and you finished the allotted time and saw no difference, would you continue to do it? Five years before I began writing this book, I was what we call "born again." I still had one huge problem: I had no idea where to go from there.

I began attending church and a Bible study group, but the group was already set. I jumped in at a time where they were just continuing as they do every week. I never had a clue what anyone was talking about. I may as well have been in advanced foreign language class. I had the desire to understand the Bible, but fact was, I didn't have the ability and had no one to guide me.

I never had a clue how to use anything in the Bible until I began to read books that explained what I'd read before without understanding what I was reading. I willingly opened the Bible myself for the first time when I was eighteen years old. I was twenty-four when I was "born again." I was twenty-eight when I began to understand how to use the Bible in my own life. That's ten years I wasted because I didn't get anything out of reading the Bible.

I'm hoping that I can teach you what I have more recently learned from the Bible that I believe could have helped me through what I call a road I could have done without. When I was born again, it was like the moment I realized I was in the wrong city; the only problem was, I had no guide. After very briefly starting in the right direction, I completely headed in the wrong direction.

The answer to the question where to go from there is simple. You have to realize something: the term *born again* means you are once again like a baby, like a newborn baby.

Chapter 9

Like a Newborn Baby

*As newborn babes, desire the sincere milk of
the word, that ye may grow thereby.*

Now, if you're familiar with babies, they can't really do a whole lot on their own. One thing they can do, and they do quite well, is drink milk. As I pointed out in the last chapter, finding someone to feed you may be quite difficult, so that brings us to this very important question: What's one of the first things a baby learns to do on its own? If you're on the same page as me, the answer is hold their own bottle. I don't expect you to pick up a Bible, open it, and begin to see changes in your life right away. What I do expect you to do is what Peter says in his first book and desire to learn. First Peter 2:2 reads,

> As newborn babes, desire the sincere milk of the
> word, that ye may grow thereby.

I'm here to whip up a formula for you, but you have to hold your own bottle. I remember a time when I made a Bible study for another young believer. He looked it over, tried to answer the questions he could without a Bible handy, and then said he wanted to do it but asked me to please not be mad with him if he didn't do it right away. I told him that he owes me no explanation and that the amount of time he spends in the Word of God is between him and God. I had done all I could do. I took the time to make a Bible study for him and told him I was here to go over it with him whenever he was ready. Have you ever tried to feed a baby that isn't hungry? You push the bottle up to their mouth for them, but that only leads to louder screaming and crying. The baby begins to flail its head around, trying to get away from the bottle. Now, as bad as that sounds, have you ever seen a baby that was hungry but had nothing to eat? A crying baby that is not hungry simply has to be entertained in the right manner. The point I'm trying to make is, you can't force someone to read the Bible; but being that crying baby without food once before, I'll never turn away a believer who wants help learning the Word of God.

Have You Learned Anything Yet?

The rest of this book will pretty much be me attempting to teach others what I wish I had learned five years ago when I truly began craving spiritual milk. I'm about to start showing you how to whip up a formula that you're about to realize I've been feeding to you since you opened this book. If my book does what it is supposed to, when you close this book you'll be heading to start concocting your own formula.

Just because you once had to become like a newborn baby, you have to remember something. Babies grow fast, but before they are mature adults capable of living on their own, they become kids. What do kids do almost to the point that it becomes irritating to most adults? If you think like me, you said, "Ask questions." Something that Peter did more than the rest of the disciples was asking questions. I'd like to take a few moments to take a look at a couple of the questions that Peter asked.

Matthew 15:15. "Then answered Peter and said unto him, Declare unto us this parable." So Jesus had just spoken to the people in a parable in which he said that it's not what goes into a man that makes him unclean; it's what comes out of him. Jesus gave this as an answer to a question the Pharisees asked about why the disciples ate without washing their hands.

Luke 12:41. "Then Peter said unto him, Lord, speakest thou this parable unto us, or even to all?" Jesus had just given another parable, and Peter simply asked if it was only for him and the other disciples, or if it was for everyone. Your question doesn't have to be anything special. It simply has to be something you don't know the answer to.

I was only trying to make a simple point here. You have to ask questions to ensure you're learning what the instructor is trying to teach. The problem with learning from books is that you don't have the one doing the teaching available for questions. Now, I mentioned one thing that a baby can learn to do, but now I want to teach you a very important lesson that the Bible teaches.

Circumcising the Heart

What is one of the first things a doctor does to a newborn baby? If you said the same thing as me, you said, "Circumcision." Genesis 17:9–14 reads,

> And God said unto Abraham, Thou shalt keep my covenant therefore, thou, shalt keep my cov-

enant therefore, thou, and thy seed after thee in their generations. This is my covenant, which ye shall keep, between me and you and thy seed after thee; Every man child among you shall be circumcised. And ye shall circumcise the flesh of your foreskin; and it shall be a token of the covenant betwixt me and you. And he that is eight days old shall be circumcised among you, every man child in your generations, he that is born in the house, or bought with money of any stranger, which is not of thy seed. He that is born in thy house, and he that is bought with thy money, must need be circumcised: and my covenant shall be in your flesh for an everlasting covenant. And the uncircumcised man child whose flesh of his foreskin is not circumcised, that soul shall be cut off from his people; he hath broken my covenant.

I first must point out the words written by Paul in his epistle to the Romans. Romans 2:25–29 reads,

> For circumcision verily profiteth, if thou keep the law: but if thou be a breaker of the law, thy circumcision is made uncircumcision. Therefore if the uncircumcision keep the righteousness of the law, shall not his uncircumcision be counted for circumcision? And shall not uncircumcision which is by nature, if it fulfill the law, judge thee, who by the letter and circumcision dost transgress the law? For he is not a Jew, which is one outwardly; neither is that circumcision,

> which is outward in the flesh: but he is a Jew,
> which is one inwardly; and circumcision is that
> of the heart, in the spirit, and not in the letter;
> whose praise is not of men, but of God.

So what Paul just told us is that a true circumcision comes within, as we cut off any wickedness from our hearts. Remember the words spoken by David just before he decided to fight Goliath. First Samuel 17:26 includes the words,

For who is this uncircumcised Philistine, that he should defy the armies of the living God?.

The words I'm hoping you caught are *uncircumcised Philistine*. Back then, it was a big deal for you to not be circumcised. It meant you weren't one of God's people. Consider that with Paul's newly revealed meaning of the term *circumcision*. Anyone can claim to be circumcised, but only God knows if our heart is truly circumcised and if we truly are one of his people. The closest we as humans can come to knowing if a human has had a true heart circumcision are the words spoken by Jesus. Luke 6:43–44 reads,

> For a good tree bringeth not forth corrupt fruit;
> neither doth a corrupt tree bring forth good
> fruit For every tree is known by his own fruit.

I want to also point out the words Paul wrote in Philippians 1:15–18:

> Some indeed preach Christ even of envy and
> strife; and some also of good will: the one preach
> Christ of contention, not sincerely, supposing
> to add affliction to my bonds: but the other of
> love, knowing that I am set for the defence of

the gospel. What then? Notwithstanding, every way, whether in pretence, or in truth, Christ is preached; and I therein do rejoice, yea, and will rejoice.

Paul just said that people are doing the right things but for the wrong reason. But the problem with that is, when you're doing the right things for the wrong reasons, you're only fooling other humans, not God. Galatians 1:10 reads,

For do I now persuade men, or God? Or do I seek to please men? For if I yet pleased men, I should not be the servant of Christ.

Rahab went against her own people to help the Israelites, simply because she feared God. Just think of what could have happened to her had her people found out that she was hiding the spies before they had a chance to overtake the land. This is a great example of someone who did what was considered wrong but for the right reason. The only thing that was keeping her from doing the right thing for the right reason is the fact that she wasn't an Israelite at the time, and she actually betrayed her own people. We now have the benefit of living in a time where we are all considered God's people.

Peter Understands

In Acts chapter 10, Peter had a dream of a number of animals that were considered unclean. He heard a voice telling him to rise, kill, and eat. Peter did what he'd been taught all his life and replied, "Not so, Lord; for I have never eaten anything that is common or unclean." God then proceeds to tell Peter not to call anything that he has made clean, unclean. When Peter awoke, he didn't understand what this vision meant. Now, at this time, there were three men who had been sent to find Peter. Acts 10:28 reads,

> And he said unto them, Ye know how that it is an unlawful thing for a man that is a Jew to keep company, or come unto one of another nation; but God hath shewed me that I should not call any man common or unclean.

Peter, as well as many others, had to learn that what he had previously been taught no longer mattered. When Jesus healed on the Sabbath, religious leaders tried to find fault in what he did, but he gave them a very good reason for why he did it, and made sure they knew he wasn't wrong for doing so.

When you're born again, you must do the same. We've spent our whole lives learning of human wisdom, learning the ways of the world. We now have to learn of Godly wisdom and the teachings of Jesus. As I already stated, once you realize you need to change direction, you still have several wrong directions in which you can go. If you don't go in the right direction, you won't make it to your desired destination. While there are many directions we can go, ultimately there are only two destinations: heaven and hell. There are many different ways to get to hell, but Jesus tells us that the only way to heaven is through him (John 14:6).

When you became a leader in sin, you basically said that you were smart enough or capable of doing things on your own. Unfortunately, they were the wrong things. When people do what's wrong, it's usually because they think they can do it without getting caught, or at least without consequences. They think they are smarter than what could stop them. First Corinthians 3:18 reads,

> Let no man deceive himself. If any man among you seemeth to be wise in this world, let him become a fool, that he may be wise.

Those are some pretty harsh words if you think about it. But fact is, it's true. Any example I gave during my "Leaders in Sin" chapter could fall under that verse. But the examples I gave in the chapter right before it may more accurately fall under another verse. Matthew 15:14 reads,

> And if the blind lead the blind, both shall fall into the ditch.

Now, I hope that through reading this, you've been able to pinpoint times in your life when you fell victim to everything we've noticed these men and women doing. People usually do something because they have seen someone do something and think that since someone else did it, they can do it too. So why does the Bible include so many horrible stories that actually could teach someone the wrong things? Romans 15:4 reads,

> For whatsoever thing were written aforetime were written for our learning, that we through patience and comfort of the scriptures might have hope.

Have you ever played the game pin the tail on the donkey? The game where you try to connect the tail of a donkey to its body while blindfolded? Can you imagine how easy it would be if you had your eyes open with no blindfold? Having the Bible handy is almost like taking an open-book test. The problem is, most people aren't taking advantage of this tool and act like they are going into an open-book test without their book and without studying. Sometimes it truly is like we're blind and have no idea what is right in front of us, but other times, we just close our eyes and pretend we can't see it simply because we don't want to.

In the book of Acts, Jesus blinded Saul for three days and then had his eyes opened. There is no question that when Saul regained his sight, his entire life changed. It's nothing short of amazing at how different his eyes were before he lost his sight for three days. I'd say it's safe to say he took advantage of regaining his eyesight. What would you do if you realized you were blind up to this point in life and now had been given the ability to see?

CHAPTER 10

WITH OPENED EYES (WE CALL IT MUD)

Significant people recognize significant actions.

I'm going to begin this chapter by showing you something very important about sight. John 9:4–7 reads,

> As long as I am in the world, I am the light of the world. When he had thus spoken, he spat on the ground, and made clay of the spittle, and he anointed the eyes of the blind man with the clay, and said unto him, Go, wash in the pool of Siloam, (which is by interpretation Sent.) He went his way therefore, and washed and came seeing.

Wouldn't it be nice if it was that easy to finally see everything you never could see before? When Jesus spoke of the blind leading the blind, he wasn't speaking of men who literally had no visual eyesight; he was speaking of people who are teaching the wrong things unintentionally. What I want you to take special note of is what came right before that. Chapter 9 begins with,

> And as Jesus passed by, he saw a man which was blind from birth. And his disciples asked him, saying, Master, who did sin, this man, or his parents, that he was born blind? Jesus answered, Neither hath this man sinned, nor his parents: but that the works of God should be made manifest in him.

Now look at the reactions of the people who saw the previously blind man:

> The neighbours therefore, and they which before had seen him that he was blind, said, Is not this he that sat and begged? Some said, This is he: others said, He is like him: but he said, I am he. Therefore said they unto him, How were thine eyes opened? He answered and said, A man that is called Jesus made clay, and anointed my eyes, and said unto me, Go to the pool of Siloam, and wash: and I went and washed, and I received sight.

If my book, as well as any self-help or Christian-based book works the way it's supposed to, you should be able to refer to it as "clay" or "mud" in the sense it's what Jesus used when he was helping a previously blind man receive his sight. I remember a time shortly after I was born again where I began thinking things like, *I feel like I just have someone else's memories.* I couldn't believe how blind I'd been to the life that was right in front of me. I'm hoping you're already at that point and, if not, that by the time you get done with this book, you without a doubt will be. I want to include the closing words of chapter 9. John 9:39–41 reads,

> And Jesus said, For judgment I am come into this world, that they which see not might see; and that they which see might be made blind. And some of the Pharisees which were with him heard these words, and said unto him, Are we blind also? Jesus said unto them, If ye were blind, ye should have no sin: but now ye say, We see; therefore your sin remaineth.

To help strengthen the point I'm about to make, I must add another verse. Second Peter 2:21 reads,

> For it had been better for them not to have known the way of righteousness, than, after they have known it, to turn from the holy commandment delivered unto them. But the true proverb, The dog is turned to his own vomit again; and the sow that was washed to her wallowing in the mire.

Remember the difference between Adam's and David's response when they were caught in their sins. Adam told God that it was his fault because he got the fruit from the woman whom God gave him, and all David could say was that he had sinned, no excuses. Think about this as you move forward in your daily life; everything that you do is being watched by God. How many people won't litter if someone is looking, but if they are alone, the ground is just an easily accessed trash can?

Usually, when we perform a certain action or choose a certain career or lifestyle, it's because we first saw someone else doing it and thought that it looked fun, or we noticed that they were living well and we wanted to be like them. I'm sure everyone would like to make a doctor's salary, but not everyone wants to put forth the time, effort, and money that it takes to do so.

The title of this chapter is "With Opened Eyes." So what exactly do you do with opened eyes? Mark 8:22–25 reads,

> And he cometh to Bethsaida; and they bring a blind man unto him, and he besought him to touch him. And he took the blind man by the hand, and led him out of the town; and when he had spit on his eyes, and put his hands upon him, he asked him if he saw ought. And he looked up, and said, I see men as trees, walking. After that the put his hands again upon his eyes, and made him look up: and he was restored, and saw every man clearly.

So what did this man who was blind do when he received his sight? He saw every man clearly. I'm not going to be able to list every man in the Bible, but I'm not going to point out some characteristics of men from the Bible that you should then try to figure out which ones you want to be more like.

Viewing Men of the Past

If we started with Adam, I'd hope you would say you don't exactly want to be like him for reasons that we have already discussed, mainly pertaining to how he reacted when confronted by God about his sin.

Now, who wouldn't want to be like Noah? I mean, he was described as "perfect in his generations." The problem, though, is it doesn't tell us why. We didn't get to see what kind of person Noah was clearly until he had fallen to alcohol.

Who wouldn't want to be like Abraham, a man mentioned over and over, known for his amazing faith? Well, when I closely examine the life of Abraham outside of his amazing faith displayed when he was about to kill his own son, what I see is a man who lied to Pharaoh out of fear and committed adultery (even though it was at his wife's request). He then sent his own son and the mother of his child away, seeming not to care too much if they lived or died. These aren't exactly things that are appealing to me.

One thing that I did see in Abraham that I really admire is how he handled the situation with Lot when their men and possessions grew too large for the land in Genesis chapter 13. First of all, he wanted to keep peace, so he suggested to his nephew Lot that they part ways. But what he did next is even greater. He let Lot choose where he wanted to go first. He said, "You go one way, and I'll go the other." He didn't look around and pick the best place for himself first and send Lot to whatever was left.

He then followed up with two more great events. One, after Lot had been captured, he armed 318 men and went and rescued his nephew. He then pleaded to God for the life of Lot when God revealed that Lot had chosen his land very poorly just as God was about to destroy the city for its evil. If we remove the negative about Abraham as the New Testament does, what I see from Abraham is that he was a fair man, very humble, and cared about others.

As we continue down the line, let us consider Abraham's grandson Jacob, a man whom we discussed earlier and pointed out that he not only made his brother sell his birthright for a single meal, but he then proceeded to deceive his own father and steal his brother's blessing as well. Not exactly the man I want to be, but in Genesis

29:20, Jacob displays a characteristic that I feel is absolutely amazing. Genesis 29:20 reads, "And Jacob served seven years for Rachel; and they seemed unto him but a few days, for the love he had to her."

A man who impacted my life more than any other man on this earth said these words to me, "When you find a job you enjoy, you'll never have to work another day of your life." A few years ago, I read something along those same lines; it was something like, "If you are working for something you really want, it's no longer considered work." That's something I admire about Jacob. Those seven years of work seemed like only a few days to him because of how much he loved someone. That kind of love is special.

Joseph, who was one of Jacob's sons, could interpret dreams and was very wise to the point he was put in charge of nearly all Egypt after becoming a prisoner, sold by his brothers into slavery. What Joseph did that I feel more of us humans living today should try to work on is the way he forgave his brothers for what they did to him. He also displayed great self-control as he resisted his master's wife's attempt to seduce him. I read a book in which one of its main points was that we should all strive to have the integrity of Joseph.

Although I hate to leave out men such as Moses and Joshua in this portion of my book, the next men mentioned in the Bible whom I feel more humans could stand to be like are the spies whom Joshua sent. These men kept their promise to a simple prostitute they owed nothing to except to keep their word. To be able to remember their promise to someone of no real importance to the city as they were overtaking the land means that keeping their word meant a lot to them.

I think of Ruth. When her mother-in-law told her not to worry about her and go off and start a new life while she was still young enough, she wouldn't leave her. I classify that as doing what is right even when we have the right not to.

Boaz, I believe, had the mentality of, "If no one else will do it, I will." He displayed this to me when he married Ruth after first giving someone else the opportunity. David displayed this same thing when he fought Goliath after no one else would.

In the New Testament, when these men—such as Jacob, whom we clearly said did very wrong things—are spoken of, they are only remembered for the good that they did. I'm now going to change my style of writing to point out only the very simple, good things about men and women from the Bible. Telling someone what not to do only goes so far. Sometimes we need to take the advice of Peter when he said that we must not only turn away from evil but that we must also do good. First Peter 3:11 reads,

> Let him eschew evil, and do good; let him seek peace, and ensue it.

If all you learn is what not to do or whom not to be like, you're actually going nowhere. That would be like me just staying at my friend's home and never trying to return to my own home. Yes, I wouldn't have ended up farther away from home, but I also wouldn't have ever gotten back to my home, which is where I needed to go. If you're truly set on doing good, you don't have time to pursue sin. From this point on in this chapter, I'm only going to try and just focus on the positive things people have done. If you want to hear about someone who did something bad, just pick up your local newspaper and read the police reports or watch the news, which are filled with negative information. If you want to hear about positive things, keep reading this.

Doing the Small Things

David. To me, David was very obedient, not only to God but simply to his elders. Remember the old saying, "Respect your elders." David did that. David was what I call immune to discouragement. David believed in God and gave him credit for all he did. David wasn't filled with greed or power-hungry. David had the same mentality as Boaz in the sense of, "If no one else will do it, I will."

Jonathan. Jonathan was beyond loyal to his friends and stood up for what was right no matter who was telling him to do wrong.

Solomon. When Solomon could have asked for anything in the world, all he asked for was "an understanding heart to judge thy people, that I may discern between good and bad."

Peter. Peter wasn't afraid to ask questions. Peter knew he wasn't what God wanted him to be but wasn't afraid to follow Jesus and become it. Peter worked so hard that he had visible progress. Peter did what the Lord told him to do. Peter not only asked questions to understand, but if he had no one to ask, he kept what he didn't understand on his mind until he figured out what God wanted.

Paul. Paul didn't care what people thought of his past; he knew that he was now living for the Lord, and that's all that mattered.

Philip. He took the time to read the Bible with someone else to make sure they understood what they were reading.

Stephen. After being stoned to death for preaching the word, his last words were, "Lord, do not charge them with this sin."

Nathanael. Had so much integrity that when Jesus saw him coming to him, he said, "Behold an Israelite indeed, in whom is no guile"

This should formulate a list of qualities that should be desired by all men and women on earth. If you were to put all these together, you'd end up with a man who sounds like this: a human who, when there are two people and two jobs to do, picks first and chooses the harder job, not the easier one; a human who stands up for his family and friends; a human who loves so greatly that, as long as they are doing it for someone they love, they do it without complaining; a human who will forgive no matter how badly they were hurt by someone and will do anything that needs to be done, anything that God wants done, and won't let anyone tell them that they can't do something; someone who isn't a lover of money, who has the mentality that if no one else will do it, they will, as opposed to the more commonly displayed, "Well, if no one else is doing it, why should I have to?"; someone who actually cares if they are right when judging people, who stands up for what is right; someone who desires to learn the right way to live and is so serious about it that you can easily see that their efforts have been paid off; someone who realizes, no matter how bad things are, no matter what their past consisted of, they understand the truth spoken in 2 Corinthians 5:17: "Therefore if any man be in Christ, he is a new creature: old things are passed away; behold, all things are become new."

Becoming Like…

Now, of all these mentioned, perhaps I saved the most important one for last. There is one woman whom if we aren't trying to be more like and we claim to be a Christian, then we are only fooling ourselves with the title we are claiming. Who is this woman, you ask? The woman spoken of in the words written in Matthew 1:25, which include,

She had brought forth her firstborn son: and he called his name JESUS.

What Mary did that we should all try a little harder to do is bring Jesus into this world. How many people go to church on Sunday but, unless you see them there, you'd have no idea they were a Christian? Even among people you know are Christians, the Bible or Jesus's name is very rarely mentioned in the conversation.

This week alone, I've heard things that I don't care to know that I may never be able to forget. This includes things such as bus wrecks, shootings, and several other tragedies. Not once has someone come up to me and told me something about the Bible.

So much of what we learn is from other people. If I missed the end of an NBA game and saw someone who I believed knew the result, I'd ask them who won. And then, if someone was asking if anyone knew who won that game, I'd gladly tell them who won. And most likely, if the person telling me had any sort of excitement in their voice or said that a specific player had a high scoring game or something amazing happened, I'd spend extra time watching highlights or looking up the statistics of the game. How many people go through the same amount of trouble to learn something about the Bible?

If I walked into a room and said something along the lines of, "Did you hear about those two daughters who got their father drunk and raped him?" I'd have everyone's attention. But how many people would instantly know that I was referring to the Bible? How many people would think that I was being serious? How many people would proceed to look it up on the Internet out of curiosity? How many people who care absolutely nothing about sports can name at last twelve professional athletes simply because the people around them are talking about it? How many self-proclaimed Christians can name Jesus's twelve disciples? How many people can name the seven dwarves but can't name the seven deacons chosen in the book of Acts? How many people have hundreds of songs on their iPod that they know by name, but they can't name the sixty-six books in the Bible that they carry around with them and claim to read?

If you've missed the point I'm trying to make, it's that it's hard to bring Jesus into this world because very few people know anything about Jesus or other men of the Bible. Perhaps it takes someone doing something amazing to get noticed. So who are some of the men who truly did amazing things, men whom we can learn from?

CHAPTER 11

LEARN FROM THE BEST

In the previous chapter, we learned that the humans from the past who made it into the most important book in the world were more like us than some of us may think, or perhaps I could reword that statement a little and say, we have the ability to be more like them than we think. When a young basketball player begins playing basketball, he hears the words *Michael Jordan*, and he lights up. I mean, this is the greatest player in history; even the other greatest players, not just fans, will tell you without a doubt, no disputing. If you say that anyone is better than Michael Jordan, you are clearly wrong. Here's another thing I want to point out. When they begin playing basketball, they want to "be like" Michael Jordan, but once they are now in the conversation with Michael Jordan, they hate being "compared" to Michael Jordan. Michael Jordan is to basketball as Jesus is to life. There is no argument over who the greatest basketball player of all time is, but if you asked who numbers two to nine are, you could ask one hundred different experts, and the lists made may consist of similar players, but not necessarily in the same order, and not all one hundred experts would have exactly the same eight players on that list. We'll now be taking a look at some of the men who I feel did extraordinary things, and more importantly, we'll look at how they did them. Let's now turn our attention to the sixteenth book in the Bible, Nehemiah.

Nehemiah Recognizes Opportunity

> The words of Nehemiah the son of Hachaliah. And it came to pass in the month of Chisleu, in the twentieth year, as I was in Shushan the palace, that Nanani, one of my brethren, came, he and a certain men of Judah; and I asked them concerning the Jews that had escaped, which were left of the captivity, and concerning Jerusalem. And they said unto me, The remnant that are left of the captivity there in the province are in great affliction and reproach: the wall of Jerusalem also is broken down, and the gates thereof are burned with fire

So how did Nehemiah react to this tragic news?

> And it came to pass, when I heard these words, that I sat down and wept, and mourned certain days, and fasted, and prayed before the God of heaven.

One of my favorite inspirational quotes reads as follows, "Opportunities are usually disguised as hard work, so most people don't recognize them." Nehemiah was not one of those men who missed an opportunity.

> For I was the king's cupbearer. And it came to pass in the month Nisan, in the twentieth year of Artaxerxes the king, that wine was before him: and I took up the wine, and gave it unto the king. Now I had not been beforetime sad in his presence. Wherefore the king said unto me, Why is thy countenance said, seeing thou art not sick? This is nothing else but sorrow of heart. Then I was very sore afraid, and said unto the king, Let the king live forever: why should not my countenance be said, when the city, the place of my father's sepulchers, lieth waste, and the gates thereof are consumed with fire?

So how does the king handle this news that his cupbearer is not happy, and with good reason?

> Then the king said unto me, For what dost thou make request? So I prayed to the God of heaven. And I said unto thee king, If it please the king, and if thy servant have favour in thy sight, that thou wouldest send me unto Judah, unto the city of my fathers' sepulchers, that I may build it.

The king gladly agreed, asking Nehemiah how long he would be gone. Nehemiah then asked for letters to ensure he had things like access to where he was going and the lumber and supplies he needed for the incredible job he was going to be doing.

> And I arose in the night, I and some few men with me; neither told I any of what my God

had put in my heart to do at Jerusalem: neither was there any beast with me, save the best that I rode upon. And I went out by night the gate of the valley, even before the dragon well, and to the dung port, and viewed the walls of Jerusalem, which were broken down, and the gates thereof were consumed with fire.

Then said I unto them, Ye see the distress that we are in, how Jerusalem lieth waste, and the gates thereof are burned with fire: come, and let us build up the wall of Jerusalem, that we be no more a reproach. Then I told them of the hand of my God which was good upon me; as also the king's words that he had spoken unto me. And they said, *Let us rise up and build* [italics added]. So they strengthened their hands for this good work.

Now, at this time, if just getting to Judah, convincing enough men to help him, and then putting forth all the effort and labor that it took to build the walls weren't enough, look at what else they had to deal with.

When Sanballat the Horonite, and Tobiah the servant, the Ammonite, heart of it, it grieved them exceedingly there was come a man to seek the welfare of the children of Israel. (Nehemiah 2:10)

But when Sanballat the Horonite, and Tobiah the servant, the Ammonite, and Geshem the

Arabian, heard of it, they laughed us to scorn, and despised us, and said, What is this thing that ye do? Will ye rebel against the king? (Nehemiah 2:19)

What I want to take special note of, though, is Nehemiah's response in Nehemiah 2:20: "The God of heaven, he will prosper us." From this point on, any time you see words in italics, take special note of what is said.

I want to skip ahead to Nehemiah 6:15: "*So the wall was finished in the twenty and fifth day of the month Elul, in fifty and two days.*"

Nehemiah told the people that God would ensure their success, and that's exactly what happened. When you consider that it took them only fifty-two days to build what lay waste for over a hundred years, that sparks up some questions. You'd have to assume everything must have gone completely as planned—there were no troubles, and everything just worked perfect. However, that was not the case at all. Listen to these verses:

Therefore set I in the lower places behind the wall, and on the higher places, I even set the people after their families with their swords, their spears, and their bows. (Nehemiah 4:13)

And it came to pass, from that time forth, that the half of my servants wrought in the work, and the other half of them held both the spears, the shields, and the bows, and the habergeons; and the rulers were behind all the house of Judah. (Nehemiah 4:16)

I'm going to include just a little more from chapter 4:

> But when Sanballat heard that we builded the wall, he was wroth, and took great indignation, and mocked the Jews. (Nehemiah 4:1)

> Now Tobiah the Ammonite was by him, and he said, Even that which they build, if a fox go up, he shall even break down their stone wall. (Nehemiah 4:3)

Some of you reading may wonder why I gave news that in Nehemiah 6:15, the wall was built; then I went backward to 4:13 and 16, which shows that they not only had to work hard, but they had to stand ready for battle at any moment. Then I included verses 4:1 and 4:3, which show the words of the opposition and how they didn't even believe that they could build the walls anyway. So why did I show the success before showing the opposition? Well, *if any of you have ever had an idea* that you decided you'd try to bring into reality, *you at one point believed that it could be done* and envisioned it. The problem is, we don't always know what kind of problems that may arise. *What we have to try to remember are the words* that Nehemiah spoke in verse 2:20: "*The God of heaven, he will prosper us.*" Now read just the italicized words from this paragraph. It should read, "If you have ever had an idea, you at one point believed that it could be done. What we have to try to remember are the words, "The God of Heaven, he will prosper us." There is a lot more you can learn from Nehemiah, but to continue on with the message that I'm trying to deliver with this book, I'm going to close this portion of the book with these words.

Remember the five steps I gave for how Lot's oldest daughter went about her plan: (1) She justified it. (2) She planned it. (3) She removed the obstacles. (4) She did it herself. (5) She reminded her sister why they were doing it and that it was now her turn. I'm now going to break down what Nehemiah did in this same manner.

Step 1. He cared! "And I asked them concerning the Jews that had escaped, which were left of the captivity, and concerning Jerusalem" (Nehemiah 1:2).

Step 2. He prayed to God! "When I heard these words, that I sat down and wept, and mourned certain days, and fasted, and *prayed before the God of heaven*"(Nehemiah1:4, italics added).

Step 3. He found a way! "And I said unto the king, If it please the king, and if the servant have found favour in thy sight, that thou wouldest send me unto Judah" (Nehemiah 2:5).

Step 4. He assessed the situation and made sure it was possible before bring others into it! "And I arose in the night; I and some few men with me neither told I any man what my God had put in my heart to do at Jerusalem, and viewed the walls of Jerusalem, and viewed the wall, and turned back. Then said I unto them, come, and let us build up the wall of Jerusalem." (These are only chosen words between Nehemiah 2:12–17).

Step 5. They did it! Chapter 3 is dedicated to the people helping. Nehemiah displayed step 1(he cared) here in the highest degree. He took an account of everyone and what exactly they did. That was a true show of appreciation. Doesn't everyone want to feel appreciated? "So the wall was finished in 52 days" (Nehemiah 6:15).

I encourage you to read more about Nehemiah on your own, but now let us turn our attention to one of the most popular stories in the Bible, in which we will focus on the young David.

David and Goliath: David Steps Up

At the beginning of chapter 17, the men were gathered for battle, but David wasn't even part of the army. He was almost more like the waterboy as we take note of 1 Samuel 17:17:

> And Jesse said unto David his son, Take now for thy brethren an ephah of this parched corn, and these ten loaves, and run to the camp to thy brethren; and carry these ten cheeses unto the captain of their thousand, and look how thy brethren fare, and take their pledge.

Consider how the army felt about this giant Goliath, who stood forty days challenging any one fighter without anyone standing up, willing to fight for their people.

> And all the men of Israel, when they saw the man, fled from him, and were sore afraid. (1 Samuel 17:24)

So at this point, David, who wasn't even supposed to be a part of the battle, was the only man who was willing to fight Goliath.

> And David said to Saul, Let no men's heart fail because of him; thy servant will go and fight the Philistine. (1 Samuel 17:32).

Here is one of the most important lessons that I think should be learned from this story, which I don't see taught very often. Saul desperately wanted someone to fight this giant, and when someone finally was willing to stand up and fight for his people and for God's army, Saul didn't even want David to fight Goliath and definitely didn't believe he could win.

> And Saul said to David, Thou art not able to go against this Philistine to fight with him: for thou art but a youth, and he a man of war from his youth. (1 Samuel 17:34)

I think everyone at some point in their life has been a victim of what we just saw here: David being told he couldn't do something that he obviously believed he could do, or he wouldn't have ever even instituted the idea. Sometimes we're told we're not big enough, not smart enough, not— and I'm sure you could fill in the blank with your own word. And the unfortunate thing is, sometimes we need others to believe in us for us to even have the opportunity to prove that we indeed can do what people have our minds set on. But I believe the more unfortunate thing is when we let people tell us that we can't do something that we believe we can do, and we believe them instead of ourselves and God. I don't know about you, but I can think of a few times in my life where I never even attempted something I believed I could do simply because I didn't have anyone supporting my idea. Fortunately for the Israelites, David didn't suffer from the same character defect as me. David was what I call immune to discouragement. This was David's response to Saul:

> And David said to Saul, Thy servant kept his father's sheep, and there came a lion, and a bear, and took a lamb out of the flock: and I went out after him, and smote him, and delivered it out of his mouth: and when he arose against me, I caught him by his beard, and smote him, and slew him. Thy servant slew both the lion

and the bear: and this uncircumcised Philistine shall be as one of them, seeing he hath defied the armies of the living God.

So what just happened was an oversized warrior from the Philistines stood up and challenged any fighter from the children of Israel, in which there was more than just a prize at stake—it was their freedom, something their ancestors wandered in the wilderness forty years trying to attain. With that said, not one fighter who was supposed to be in the fight stood up to fight for the army of the living God until David, whom—even when he finally stood up to accept the challenge—nobody believed in, until he spoke these very important words to Saul:

The Lord that delivered me out of the paw of the lion, and out of the paw of the bear, he will deliver me out of the hand of the Philistine. (Nehemiah 17:37)

Now let's see what Saul says to the young man he just said was too young and unskilled in battle to fight this giant.

Go and the Lord be with thee. (1 Samuel 17:37)

So what we just witnessed was the fact that even though Saul didn't necessarily believe in David, he believed in God, but David believed in himself from the beginning simply because of the fact that he himself believed in God and knew that God was with him. David was basically saying something along the lines of, "You guys have no idea what I'm capable of." And one of my newer favorite Bible verses is written in John 14:1: "Let not your heart be troubled: ye believe in God, believe also in me." Can't you almost insert that verse here into David's words: "If you believe in God, believe in me"! Say it with me—"If you believe in God, believe in me." Don't you just feel better saying that? Well, perhaps not, but remember those words; and someday, when the opportunity arises, it may help you overcome a challenge you may be facing.

One day, I was walking, and I wasn't feeling all that well, but I was obviously feeling well enough to be up walking around. I had just watched the new Hercules movie where one of his lines was, "Father, I believe in you. Give me strength." As I was walking, I said that to God and meant it with all my heart, so I was honestly expecting to just instantly feel better but, to my surprise, felt no different. But I clearly heard God's reply: *I can't give you what you already have.* I'll never forget that moment. How often do we fail to do something simply because we don't think we can? I was asking for strength to do what I was already doing. It never says God gave David some extra strength to defeat Goliath, and when humans tried to give him something extra, David refused because he already had everything he needed to defeat Goliath.

After David told Saul these words, Saul tried to clothe him in armor, but David didn't want to wear it because he wasn't comfortable in it. He then took it off and continued on his mission the only way he knew how. Now I want to take the time to break down what David did in a multistep process, which I've displayed twice already.

Step 1. He believed in himself.

Step 2. He had the "if no one else will do it, I will" mentality. (Consider the man whom we earlier saw as having this same mentality—Boaz. If you paid close attention to the closing words of Ruth, you'd know that Boaz was David's great-grandpa; perhaps this was where he got it from.)

Step 3. He understood that the people who doubted in him simply didn't know what he was capable of.

Step 4. He trusted not only in himself but in God.

Step 5. He did it.

So what have we seen so far from David?

When he heard that there was a man challenging and defying the armies of the living God, he volunteered. He had given anyone else who wanted to take on the challenge forty days, and enough was enough. It was time for God's power to show. Even when people doubted him and were showering him with discouraging words, he never let that affect what he knew: that God was with him and had proven it time and time again while tending to his father's sheep. Finally, talking about it wasn't enough, it was time to do it.

> Therefore David ran, and stood upon the Philistine, and took his sword and drew it out of the sheath thereof and slew him, and cut off his head therewith...And David took the head of the Philistine, and brought it to Jerusalem. (1 Samuel 17:51, 54)

I want to point out one more thing about David. All David had to do was prove himself once. After that, nobody doubted David anymore. Listen to this:

> And David went out whithersoever Saul sent him, and behaved himself wisely: and Saul set him over the men of war, and he was accepted in the sight of all the people, and also in the sight of Saul's servants. (1 Samuel 18:5)

> And whatsoever ye do, do it heartily as to the Lord, and not unto men; knowing that of the Lord ye shall receive the reward of the inheri-

tance: for ye serve the Lord Christ. (Colossians 3:23–24)

I Feel Like My Guardian Angel Has Been Held Captive

The next man I want to talk about is a man who proved something I find to be very important. If God is with you, you can excel anywhere you go. We briefly went over a young man earlier who was sold into slavery by his own family. That man was named Joseph, and to me, Joseph is a great example of how God is with us everywhere we go, as long as we stay faithful to him. Remember, Joseph's brothers wanted to kill him out of jealousy, until his brother Judah decided it was better to make a little money off him and still get him out of their lives. Genesis 39:1–3 reads,

> And Joseph was brought down to Egypt; and Potiphar, an officer of Pharaoh, captain of the guard, an Egyptian, bought him of the hands of the Ishmeelites which had brought him down thither. And the Lord was with Joseph, and he was a prosperous man; and he was in the house of his master the Egyptian. And his master saw that the Lord was with him, and that the Lord made all that he did to prosper in his hand.

I want to repeat the beginning of the second sentence: "And the Lord was with Joseph." So let me get this straight. Joseph was just sold as a slave, and the first thing they say about him is that the Lord was still with him? I kind of get mixed feelings from that statement because, with my human thinking, I want to make a statement like, "If God was with Joseph, why'd he let such a bad thing happen to him?" Joseph gave the answer to that question later on, but we'll get to that in a minute. Let's now pick up at verse 4–6 to find out for ourselves why God let Joseph be sold as a slave if he was really with him.

> And Joseph found grace in his sight, and he served him: and he made him overseer over his house, and all that he had he put into his hand. And it came to pass from the time that he made him overseer in his house, and over all the he had, that the Lord blessed the Egyptian's house for Josephs sake; and the blessing of the Lord was upon all the he had in the house, and in the field. And he left all that he had in Joseph's hand; and he knew not ought he had, save the bread which he did eat. And Joseph was a goodly person and well favoured.

What we see now is God didn't let Joseph just rot away as any other slave would. He had given him favor with his master, and now David was in charge of all of Potiphar's things. Verse 6 ends with the fact that Joseph was well-favored. But it seems like Joseph had to be cursed now because just as fast as he was made from a slave to what they called overseer in his house, now God allowed him to be thrown into prison. Starting at verse 7, Potiphar's wife tried to get Joseph to go to bed with her, but he refused. Verse 8–9 reads,

> But he refused, and said unto his master's wife, Behold, my master wotteth not what is with me in the house, and he committed all that he hath to my hand; there is none greater in this house than I; neither hath he kept back any thing

> from me but thee, because thou art his wife: how then can I do this great wickedness, and sin against God?

When Joseph rejected her, she then cried out and lied about Joseph, claiming he tried to rape her. This lie was what landed Joseph in prison. Verse 20 reads,

> And Joseph's master took him, and put him into the prison, a place where the king's prisoners were bound: and he was there in the prison.

Okay, so pretty bad luck for Joseph. Now he was sure to be just another wasted life in a prison, right? Wrong! Read verse 21:

> But the Lord was with Joseph. [Wait a second, did you read what I just read? Joseph was just thrown in prison, and the very next statement is that the "Lord is with him"? Now this whole having-God-on-your-side thing is getting confusing.] And shewed him mercy, and gave him favour in the sight of the keeper of the prison.

It then goes on to say that the keeper of the prison committed to Joseph's hand all the prisoners who were in the prison; and whatsoever they did there, he was the doer of it. Then the last words of chapter 39 are, "And that which he did, *the Lord made it prosper.*"

So I want to throw a few things at you real quick. Joseph was sold to the Ishmaelites to become a slave. He was bought as a slave by Potiphar, but in verse 4, it says that he "served" him. Now I recently read in a book that there is a very big difference between being a servant and a slave. What stuck out more than anything was that a slave does something because he has to while a servant does something because he wants to. So if I apply it to this situation we've just read about and try to better *understand what God wants me to learn from it,* this is what I've come up with. Unless we are completely alone, there is always someone watching. Now, since Joseph was acting more like a servant than a slave, this got the attention of men of authority. I'm sure at any company, you can see a difference between one man to the next in how he fulfills his duties. Is he acting like a slave who does the minimal work to get by, or does he act like a servant who is enjoying the same duties as a slave who hates it? It wasn't what Joseph was doing; it was how he was doing it. Joseph could have given up. He could have cried out to God, "Why me?" I mean, all this happened because of the dreams he had that told the future he would have because of God. But instead, Joseph showed that he was worthy of what was shown to him in his dreams. Now Joseph was about to be given an amazing opportunity.

Chapter 40 begins with two men being thrown into prison. One was the butler of the king of Egypt, and the other was the king's baker. Both of them had dreams, and Joseph interpreted them. After hearing the butler's dream, Joseph told him that he would be restored to his place and asked one small favor. Genesis 40:14 reads,

> But think on me when it shall be well with thee, and shew kindness, I pray thee, unto me, and make mention of me unto Pharaoh, and bring me out of this house.

Unfortunately for Joseph, the butler was more like most humans and—in what I'll accredit to his excitement of his own freedom, which came out as selfishness—forgot all about Joseph. Genesis 40:23 reads,

> Yet did not the chief butler remember Joseph,
> but forgat him.

Now, if Joseph was like me, he probably thought for sure that was his opportunity to finally be set free, which was something he deserved since he was never guilty of what he was thrown in prison for; but once again, it seemed like God was just completely ignoring Joseph, even though the Bible keeps reminding us that he was with him the whole time. But here is where everything changes. Chapter 41 begins with Pharaoh himself having disturbing dreams, dreams for which he sent and called all the magicians and wise men of Egypt, but no one could interpret this dream. Finally, the butler told Pharaoh about Joseph, who interpreted his dream accurately, and immediately, Pharaoh sent for Joseph. Joseph interpreted Pharaoh's dream, telling him that it means there would be seven years of great plenty followed by seven years of famine, which would be so bad that they'd forget all about the good years. Joseph then told Pharaoh how to handle this situation. Verses 34–35 read:

> Let Pharaoh do this, and let him appoint officers over the land, and him appoint officers over the land, and take up the fifth part of the land of Egypt in the seven plenteous years. And let them gather all the food of those good years that come, and lay up corn under the hand of Pharaoh, and let them keep food in the cities.

So Joseph told Pharaoh that what he must do was save 20 percent of everything they got in the good years to save for the bad years. Now, anyone who has failed at something knows sometimes a good idea isn't good enough; it has to be *well executed*. Choosing someone capable of seeing this out was as important to Pharaoh as having the plan itself.

Kobe Bryant made twenty-five million dollars in the 2015–2016 season. Twenty-five million athletes around the world played more basketball than him and didn't get paid a dime—actually, you could even go on to say that twenty-five million athletes paid to play basketball. It's not the fact that Kobe Bryant was playing basketball; it was how he played basketball. He was drafted in 1996, thirteenth overall. More times than not, the thirteenth pick is lucky to ever make an all-star game or even be a notable starter. Kobe retired this year and is going down as one of the greatest players to ever live. Twelve teams passed up on Kobe Bryant, and the team that actually had the sense to draft him ended up trading him moments later before he ever played a single game for them. Kobe Bryant accomplished the ultimate goal that the NBA has to offer five times as he won NBA championships. He came in second twice. Kobe Bryant just became the first player in NBA history to play twenty seasons with the same team. That means 25 percent of his career, he won a championship, and over 33 percent, he made it to the championship. There are so many players who have been chosen first overall and never even made it to a championship, let alone win one. The point I'm trying to make is the importance of choosing the best man for the job.

Let's continue reading chapter 41:37–40:

> And the thing was good in the eyes of Pharaoh, and in the eyes of all his servants. And Pharaoh said unto his servants, Can we find such a one as this, a man in whom the Spirit of God is? And Pharaoh said unto Joseph Forasmuch as God hath shewed thee all this, there is none so discreet and wise as thou art: thou shalt be over my house, and according unto thy word shall all

> my people be ruled: only in the throne will I be greater than thou.

Pharaoh could have chosen anyone to do this. He was the king, so why did he choose a prisoner? It wasn't that Joseph was a prisoner; it was *how Joseph handled himself* while he was in prison.

I don't know how much money Kobe Bryant made in 1996, which is the year he was drafted, but the most recent number thirteenth pick made about two million dollars this season, and I think it's safe to say that twenty years ago, Kobe would have made less than that. The minimum salary for NBA players, I believe, is somewhere around five hundred thousand dollars. So it's not just that Kobe was an NBA player; it's how he handled himself while he was in the NBA.

Joseph went on to complete his task and was even reunited with his family after his father sent his brothers to Egypt to buy food after hearing that they had the only food around. The last thing I want to include about Joseph is his response to his brothers. Genesis 45:5 reads,

> I am Joseph your brother, whom ye sold into Egypt. Now therefore be not grieved, nor angry with yourselves, that ye sold me hither: for God did send me before you to preserve life.

So it finally makes sense. God used Joseph to save his people. Had Joseph not been sold by his brothers, there would have been no one to interpret Pharaoh's dream, which was the only warning they got about the upcoming famine. Joseph was also needed to tell them how to deal with it. Romans 8:28 says, "We know that all things work together for good to them that love God, to them who are called according to his purpose." Joseph's story is one of the best examples of that verse.

Daniel's Wisdom

Ezekiel 28: 3 reads,

> Behold, thou art wiser than Daniel; there is no secret that they can hide from thee.

Knowing that verse, I find it very hard to consider not including a little about Daniel in this. Daniel 1:3–5 reads,

> And the king spake unto Ashpenaz the master of his eunuchs, that he should bring certain of the children of Israel, and of the king's seed, and of the princes; children in whom was no blemish, but well favoured, and skillful in all wisdom, and cunning in knowledge, and understanding science, and such as had ability in them to stand in the king's palace, and whom they might teach the learning and the tongue of the Chaldeans And the king appointed them a daily provision of the king's meat, and of the wine which he drank: so nourishing them three years, that at the end thereof they might stand before the king.

Among these men were Daniel and three of his friends. Now Daniel decided to make a little request of his own:

> But Daniel purposed in his heart that he would not defile himself with the portion of the king's meat, nor with the wine which he drank: there-

fore he requested of the prince of the eunuchs
that he might defile himself.

The prince of the eunuchs told Daniel that he was afraid to grant Daniel's request because if the king noticed they were not getting as healthy as the other children, it could put his life in danger. Daniel didn't want to eat food that was offered to other gods, so Daniel did what is key in all situations that could possibly require a negotiation to please both parties involved.

> Prove thy servants, I beseech thee, ten days; and let them give us pulse to eat, and water to drink. Then let our countenances be looked upon before thee, and the countenance of the children that eat of the portion of the king's meat: and as thou seest, deal with thy servants.

So Daniel was chosen among other young men to come prove themselves worthy to be the king's advisors. Daniel could have eaten anything he wanted, but he chose to eat healthy. Don't you want to be as healthy as possible to do what God wants you to do?

In chapter 2, Nebuchadnezzar had a disturbing dream and called all the magicians, astrologers, and sorcerers to come interpret it, but no one could do it. This angered the king to the point he planned to kill everyone. Look how Daniel handled this situation in Daniel 2:17–18. After going to the king and requesting a little more time, he went to Hananiah, Mishael, and Azariah "that they would desire mercies of heaven concerning this secret; that Daniel and his fellows should not perish with the rest of the wise men of Babylon."

Daniel completely relied on God. James 1:5 says that if anyone lacks wisdom, ask God.

After Daniel gave Nebuchadnezzar the interpretation of his dream and told him that his kingdom would be taken from him, Daniel then gave him some advice and told him to repent. Daniel 4:27 reads,

> Wherefore, O king, let my counsel be acceptable unto thee, and break off thy sins by righteousness, and thine iniquities by shewing mercy to the poor; if it may be a lengthening of thy tranquility.

Daniel not only told the king to repent but also told him how to. So often we tell someone what not to do but don't tell them what to do. The Bible says to turn away from evil *and* do good. That tells me that turning away from evil isn't good enough. Think about dealing with children. So often they start doing something we don't like, and we yell at them to stop. And finally they stop, but five minutes later, they are doing something else, which leads to the exact same reaction. Sometimes it's as simple as telling someone what to do, which can mean the difference in the outcome of a situation. Sometimes!

This next verse tells you exactly how great Daniel was. Daniel 6:3–4 reads,

> Then this Daniel was preferred above the presidents and princes, because an excellent spirit was in him; and the king thought to set him over the whole realm. Then the presidents and princes sought to find occasion against Daniel concerning the kingdom; but they could not find none occasion nor fault; forasmuch as he

was faithful, neither was there any error or fault found in him.

When people are desperately looking for a way to criticize you but can't, that says a lot about someone. They couldn't even make up a believable lie about Daniel. They actually tricked the king into signing a decree that says if a person prayed to God, he would be thrown into a den of lions to be killed Daniel 6:11 reads:

> Then these men assembled, and found Daniel praying and making supplication before his God.

I've been hearing a lot of preaching on the fear of the Lord. Well, how about this? Instead of focusing on "fear of the Lord," why not preach on *trusting* in the Lord? Fearing the Lord entails you are doing something wrong, and the fear of the Lord is like a scared straight tactic. But trusting in the Lord is what we should aim for. Aim for getting to a place in our life where we no longer fear God but trust that God will be there for us because we are doing the right things. Daniel told King Nebuchadnezzar he needed to fear God; Daniel was never in fear of losing anything. Humans tried to threaten his life, but there was no fear in Daniel. First John 4:18 says that perfect love expels all fear; meaning, if you love God and do what he wants you to do, you should no longer have to fear him. You can trust him. This is actually a great way to test if what you're doing is right, or simply to check the status of your relationship with God. After Nebuchadnezzar was removed from his throne, a new king, Darius, took his place. Listen to Darius's words to Daniel after he realized he had made the wrong decision in signing the decree and tried to figure out a way to save Daniel. Daniel 6:16 reads,

> Then the king commanded, and they brought Daniel, and cast him into the den of lions. Now the king spake and said unto Daniel, Thy God whom thou servest continually, he will deliver thee.

Did you read what I just read, that Darius ordered Daniel to be thrown into the lions' den, and all he could say to him was that God will protect him? What I really like about this story is the fact that Daniel's wisdom and faithfulness to God, and the way he gave God all the credit for his understanding and interpretations, made a believer out of Darius.

I wrote a small piece I titled "Soul Saving 101." James 5:20 had become my favorite Bible verse, and I wanted to know more about it and how to get better at it. I looked to whom I have to believe is the greatest soul saver of all time and then how he did it. I noticed another verse about souls. In Proverbs 11:30, it says that he who "winneth" souls is "wise." So I had to change course for a minute. How do you "win" something? The answer I came up with is that you have to get the voters' attention. Jesus got Peter's attention when he took a failure of a fishing trip and then made it into the most successful fishing trip Peter had probably ever been on. Daniel is said to be wise, and over and over again, he impressed people by letting God use him to do so.

God sent the angel Gabriel to help him understand on several occasions. But look how Daniel got his understanding on at least one occasion. Daniel 8:27 reads,

> And I Daniel fainted, and was sick certain days; afterward I rose up, and did the king's business; and I was astonished at the vision, but none understood it.

Daniel 9:2 reads,

> In the first year of his reign I Daniel understood by the books the number of the years, whereof the word of the Lord came to Jeremiah the prophet, that he would accomplish seventy years in the desolations.

Daniel got his understanding from simply reading the same scriptures we have available to us today. How often, when faced with a certain situation, do we question or wonder why this is happening to us, and we do not understand why God could be doing something? Well, if you don't know the scriptures and how God works, you'll never understand. I can look back on my life and make amazing comparisons between events in my life and things that happened to other men in the Bible. After seeing their reasons, I can easily say that God could have been doing that in my life as well. Whether I'm right or wrong, I can't say for sure, but I can tell you that I has helped me come to peace with those misfortunes, and I no longer blame or question God for my times of distress.

Of all the things that Daniel did, perhaps one of the most meaningful, I'm going to close this portion of my book with this statement, which is from chapter 6 verse 10, when Daniel heard that if he prayed to God, he'd be thrown into the lion's den:

> Now when Daniel knew that the writing was signed, he went home. And in his room with his windows open toward Jerusalem he knelt down on his knees three times that day, and prayed and gave thanks before his God, as was his custom since early days.

Remember when he was told to eat food and drink wine straight from the king's own kitchen, and he said he didn't want to defile himself. He had to negotiate by saying to test him for ten days, and if he didn't look healthier than the other men, then he would eat the food they offered him. When it came to food, he was willing to negotiate, but when it came to God, there was no negotiating. He simply went on with his daily prayers, showing that nothing was going to interfere with his relationship to God.

04582 Treatment—Just Try It

I'm about to share with you something I believe with all my heart. Matthew 5:28 reads,

> But I say unto you, That whosoever looketh on a woman to lust after her hath committed adultery with her already in his heart.

So we just heard that just thinking about a woman—not actually going through with any actual actions other than thoughts that no one else in the world even knows about, not even the woman whom you are thinking about—is just as bad as committing adultery. Well, what I believe I did that pleased God greatly before I even knew it was I simply thought about doing good things. I had gotten to a point where I felt I had help getting to what I felt was a good place in my life, and I decided it was time to simply pay it forward. Romans 15:1 reads,

> We then that are strong ought to bear the infirmities of the weak, and not to please ourselves.

I tried to do several small things, things that I never actually got to do; but now, looking back, I believe it pleased God so much that he decided I could do much more than the simple thoughts I had. Remember the parable of the talents. God gives us jobs according to our abilities. I highly encourage you to spend a certain amount of time thinking positive thoughts that would please God. I actually gave this a name; I call it *04582 treatment*. The 04 comes from 40 backward, which is Matthew's order in the sequence of books in the Bible. Then chapter 5, and then 82 is 28 backward. Basically, you are doing the opposite of what it says in Matthew 5:28. I just figured if thinking bad intentions displeases God even if you don't act on them, why wouldn't good intentions please God even if you didn't get to act on them? However, don't get that confused with me saying that you don't have to. I'm saying that before you make something a reality, you should first think it over. I'd also like to think that the more you think about an idea, the better you can make it; and when the opportunity comes, you'll be more prepared to make it a reality as good as possible. I'm going to share with you a quote by T. E. Lawrence:

> All men dream but not equally. Those who dream by night in the dusty recesses of their minds, wake in the day to find that it was vanity: but the dreamers of the day are dangerous men, for they may act on their dreams with open eyes, to make them possible.

We can't necessarily control our thoughts, or at least our initial thought. But we can control what we think about. Then if we work hard enough, we can realize what areas we still are having negative thoughts appear first, and we can continue to catch them and begin to correct them. And hopefully, in time, we can actually get to a point where the first initial thought is changed to positive.

Growing up, I was a picky eater. You could name dozens of healthy foods, and I would have an extremely negative thought, sometimes to the point I'd cry and throw a huge fit rather than eat them. Now those same foods, if you mention them, my thoughts are almost the opposite. Those thoughts changed because I did something to change them. While you begin to think about your life and what you could do to please God, remember James 1:22: "But be ye doers of the word, and not hearers only deceiving your own selves." Then ask yourself one simple question.

The harvest is plenteous, but the laborers are few.

CHAPTER 12

IS SUNDAY CHURCH ENOUGH?

So when they had dined, Jesus saith to Simon Peter, Simon, son of Jonas, lovest thou me more than these? He saith unto him, Yea, Lord; thou knowest that I love thee. He saith unto him, Feed my lambs. He saith to him again the second time, Simon, son of Jonas, lovest thou me? He saith unto him, Yea, Lord; thou knowest that I love thee. He saith unto him, Feed my sheep. He saith unto him the third time, Simon, son of Jonas, lovest thou me? Peter was grieved because he said unto him the third time, Lovest thou me? And he said unto him, Lord, thou knoest all things; thou knowest that I love thee. Jesus saith unto him, Feed my sheep.
—John 21:15–17

After Jesus was crucified and had risen from the dead, he appeared to his disciples. At the time of this appearance, Peter decided to go fishing, and some of the other disciples decided to go with him. John 21:1–3 reads,

> After these things Jesus shewed himself again to the disciples at the sea of Tiberias; and on this wise shewed he himself. There were together Simon Peter, and Thomas called Didymus, and Nathanael of Cana in Galilee, and the sons of Zebedee, and two other of his disciples. Simon Peter saith unto them, I go a fishing. They say unto him, We also go with thee. They went forth, and entered into a ship immediately; and that night they caught nothing.

This is probably one of the most meaningful chapters in the entire Bible, to me at least. Without this chapter, I believe the entire book of Acts may not exist. This is a great example of what happens to us the moment we leave church. For a lot of people, church is something you do on Sunday, whether you want to or not; but after church, it's back to whatever life you want to live. It's amazing how many people only attend church on Christmas and Easter. The disciples almost suffered from this very thing.

Once Jesus was no longer right by Peter's, as well as the other disciples', side, they went back to what they knew before Jesus came into their life. Remember what Peter was doing when Jesus first called him? Peter had once again returned to fishing, but Jesus wasn't about to let all his work go to waste.

Jesus called Peter aside and asked him three times if he loved him. Each time after Peter declared he indeed loved Jesus, he gave him an instruction, the same instruction over and over. Jesus told Peter to "feed his sheep"; in other words, to teach others what Jesus taught him. Romans 15:1–2 reads,

> We then that are strong ought to bear the infirmities of the weak, and not to please ourselves.

> Let every one of us please his neighbor for his
> good to edification.

I'm going to go ahead and give you the answer to the question asked in the title of this chapter—NO! Sunday church is where it starts, and if you are finishing where you start without ever moving, what are you really doing? I'm not trying to put down anyone for going to church because, unfortunately, there are a lot of people who do simply make it to church on Sunday morning but never really try to get involved in any other way and, for churches that have multiple services throughout the week, never really even make an attempt at attending multiple services. To them, the answer is simple—yes, Sunday church is enough.

Just before I was born again, I decided to go to church where I hadn't gone to seven years. To me, church was nothing more than a place that families go to on Sunday. I believed in God, I feared God, but I definitely didn't have a real relationship with him. Honestly, looking back, I'm shocked that I even went to church considering my initial reason. But once I was there, I couldn't see myself anywhere else.

I grew up Catholic, so I went to the Catholic Church. Actually, the first morning that I went wasn't even on a Sunday. When I had the idea, my intentions were simply to go on Sunday. I had no intentions of taking it any further than that, but before I knew it, I was attending church several days in a row.

I basically went there to pray in the morning. Living in a small town, and living only about a mile from the church, it was absolutely nothing to get up in the morning and make it to church. From the first morning I went, I went ten days in a row. On the third day, I was "born again."

Growing up Catholic, not ever reading the Bible or listening to any sort of preaching, I didn't even know that I was born again that day until much later, but now I can clearly look back on that day and say that it was the day I was born again. From that day forward, I knew that, for me, Sunday church would never be "enough."

I grew up in a family where I had to go to church every Sunday or close to it, but other than a few prayers here and there, Sunday church was definitely "enough." And unfortunately, that seems to be true for many families. And for some people, that is perfectly fine. Don't think by any means I am saying that everyone who claims to be a Christian has to go on mission trips or feel bad for missing church on a Wednesday night after they had attended church three times a week for forty-three weeks previous. Matthew 25:14–30 reads,

> For the kingdom of heaven is as a man travelling into a far country, who called his own servants, and delivered them his goods. And unto one he gave five talents, to another two, and to another one; to every man according to his several ability; and straightway took his journey. Then he that had received the five talents went and traded with the same, and made them other five talents. And likewise he that had received two, he also gained other two. But he that had received one went and digged in the earth, and hid his lord's money. After a long time the lord of those servanted cometh, and reconeth with them. And so he that had revived five talents came and brought other fie talents, saying, Lord, thou deliveredst unto me five talents: behold, I have gained beside them five talents more. His lord said unto him, Well done, thou good and faithful servant: thou hast been faithful over a few things, I will make thee

ruler over many things: enter thou into the joy of thy lord. He also that had reveived two talents came and said, Lord, thou deliveredst unto me two talents: behold, I have gained two other talents beside them. His lord said unto him, Well done, good and faithful servant; thou hast been faithful over a few things, I will make thee ruler over many things: enter thou into the joy of thy lord. Then he which had received the one talent came and said, Lord, I knew thee that thou art an hard man, reaping where thou hast not sown, and gathering where thou hast not strawed: and I was afraid, and went and hid they talent in the earth: lo, there thou hast that is thine. His lord answered and said unt him, Thou wicked and slothful servant, thou knowest that I reap where I sowed not, and gather where I have not strawed: thou oughtest therefore to have put my money to the exchangers, and then at my coming I should have received mine own with usury. Take therefore the talent from him, and give it unto him which hath ten talents. For unto every one that hath shall be given, and he shall have abundance: but from him that hath not shall be taken away even that which he hath.

This parable demonstrates the fact that there are different levels of seriousness and dedication when it comes to being a Christian. This story begins with a man who was about to leave his home. He decided to leave his possessions with his servants so that while he was gone, they could make him more.

He gave each of his three servants "talents" according to his own ability. The church consists of different parts. There are pastors who lead the church. Obviously, we have to say that pastors would probably be considered more like the man who was given the five talents. Outside of the pastor, we have people who play instruments, sing, lead classes such as Bible studies, and of course, the ones who attend those extra activities. Let's just say those are the ones given two talents.

That only leaves one part of the church left. They are the ones who have been going to church every Sunday week in and week out but never really make any extra effort to do something outside of church that isn't first seeking their own pleasure instead of intending to help someone else somehow, someway. These people are like the man given one talent.

Look at how he responded to the two servants given five and two talents. One gained five more, and the other only gained two more. But the response was the same: "Well done, good and faithful servant." It doesn't matter what you're doing as long as you're doing something according to your own abilities.

When I went to church ten days in a row, I couldn't look to the guy beside me and say, "Why aren't you going to church?" Four months later, I couldn't even make it to church at times because my schedule changed. I was simply doing what I was capable of doing. Now look at the servant given only one talent. He hid his talent, and upon the Lord's return, he took his talent and gave it to the one who had already been given five talents. I'm sure if anyone reading this is one of the people who attend church every week and feel they are a good person and have found ways to justify why they aren't doing more, they may be offended by that statement, but let me point out something. There are plenty of men who weren't even given one talent; those men weren't even there. That has to be considered the people not even going to church at all. By logic, you have to assume that by showing up to church, you are saying you want to be a servant; but if you don't ever increase and do more, you are obviously wasting the talent God gave you. One of the most important things I've ever heard is that there is someone out there whom only you can reach.

I can do all things through Christ who strengthens me.
—Philippians 4:13

CHAPTER 13

UNLESS YOU TRY

*He who has the ability to take action has
the responsibility to take action.*
—Nicholas Cage, *National Treasure*

Mark Eaton

There was a man who stood seven feet four inches tall. He hated basketball. He didn't even like to hear the word *basketball* because he tried to play in high school and wasn't any good. Since he was so tall, he was constantly being asked if he played basketball, which only irritated him because he had tried and wasn't any good at it. One day, while working as a mechanic, a college basketball coach walked in, and seeing his height, the coach knew he had a chance to do something special with this man. He knew that sliding under cars was wasting the gift God gave him. He asked the young man if he played basketball and tried to persuade him to come practice with him, but the man refused over and over. Finally, due to the coach's persistence, he finally gave in, figuring once he saw how horrible he was, the coach would leave him alone, and he could go on with his life. That man became an NBA all-star.

You see, his previous coaches simply didn't know how to use him properly. The college coach who walked in knew exactly how to use him. Sometimes knowing how to get the most out of what we already have is just as important as simply having the incredible gift or ability. I'd like to think that our previous "coaches" have been the people in our lives up to this point, the ones we earlier learned actually "deceived" us or led us astray blindly. But at some point, if you finally accept the offer from the right coach and let God show you how to get the most out of what you already have, you can finally live up to your potential. God's offer has been on the table since we were born, but at what point do we finally accept?

Just Take That First Step

In the last chapter, we established that Sunday church is where it starts, but it shouldn't be where you stay. So now comes the important question: When do you begin to "do more"? At what point, after deciding that Sunday church isn't enough, do you actually begin to venture out into new territory? When do you become what the Bible defines as a "laborer"? Ecclesiastes 11:4 reads,

> He that observeth the wind shall not sow; and
> he that regardeth the clouds shall not reap.

At some point after you have the thought to do more, you just have to try. Even if you can think of a couple reasons why you shouldn't, you just have to trust that if what you're doing is for God, he won't let you fail. Remember the old saying, "You'll never know unless you try"?

When you first have these desires, they will also come with doubts and opposing thoughts as to why you can't or shouldn't do them. You just have to remember that if what you're doing is for God, he wants you to succeed and will make sure that happens. When God told Abraham to offer his son Isaac as an offering, when Isaac noticed there was no lamb, he asked Abraham about it, and Abraham said that God would provide it. At this time, Abraham just didn't have the heart to tell Isaac that he indeed was the offering. Abraham never really lied, but once he no longer had to offer Isaac, it did sort of become a lie. God made sure Abraham's word stayed good. Genesis 22:13 reads,

> And Abraham lifted up his eyes and looked, and behold behind him a ram caught in a thicket by his thorns and Abraham went and took the ram, and offered him up for a burnt offering in the stead of his son.

Moses was chosen for one of the most important tasks in the Bible. God had made a promise to Abraham, a promise that was meant for his descendants and took hundreds of years to keep. When Moses was told he would be the man to lead the Israelites out of slavery in Egypt to the Promised Land, he was far from confident and excited. Exodus 3:7–10 reads,

> And the Lord said, I have surely seen the affliction of my people which are in Egypt, and have heard their cry by reason of their taskmasters; for I know their sorrows; and I am come down to deliver them out of the hand of the Egyptians, and to bring them up out of that land unto a good land and a large, unto a land

flowing with milk and honey, unto the place of the Canaanites and the Hittites, and the Amorites, and the Perizzites, and the Hivites, and the Jebusites. Now therefore, behold, the cry of the children of Israel is come unto me: and I have also seen the oppression wherewith the Egyptians oppress them. Come now therefore, and I will sent thee unto Pharaoh, that thou mayest bring forth my people the children of Israel out of Egypt.

Listen to Moses's response in the following verse:

And Moses said unto God, Who am I, that I should go unto Pharaoh, and that I should bring forth the children of Israel out of Egypt?

So what we just heard was God telling Moses to do something and Moses doubting that he has the ability or authority to do so, but listen to God's response in verse 12:

And he said, Certainly I will be with thee; and this shall be a token unto thee, that I have sent thee: When thou hast brought forth the people out of Egypt, ye shall serve God upon this mountain.

God just told Moses that he was guaranteeing him success, and to prove it, he was giving him a token. Remember the first time God gave something as a token? Let me refresh your memory. Genesis 9:13 reads:

> I do set my bow in the cloud, and it shall be for a token of a covenant between me and the earth.

That's a token of the promise he made to never again flood the earth, which we still see to this day. God now has just promised Moses success, but listen to Moses's response just a few chapters later. Exodus 4:10 reads,

> And Moses said unto the Lord, O my Lord, I am not eloquent, neither heretofore, nor since thou hast spoken unto thy servant: but I am slow of speech, and of a slow tongue.

Moses just told God that he isn't even fit for this because he isn't a great speaker. Exodus 4:13 reads,

> And he said, O my Lord, send, I pray thee, by the hand of him whom thou wilt send.

Now Moses was pleading to God to use anyone besides him. I want to skip ahead just for a moment. Deuteronomy 34:10 reads,

> And there arose not a prophet since in Israel like unto Moses, whom the Lord knew face to face, in all the signs and the wonders, which the Lord sent him to do in the land of Egypt to Pharaoh, and to all his servants, and to all his land, and in all that mighty hand, and in all the great terror which Moses shewed in the sight of all Israel.

What we've just seen is God telling someone to do something and them doubting that they could do it. Then because they went ahead and tried, even though they doubted themselves, they became not just great, but so great that the only argument that doubters had when trying to criticize Jesus was arguments based around Moses.

Moses wasn't the only one who faced a task that seemed impossible. Whether it be from yourself or from everyone else watching, there will always be opposition to a task done for God. In 1 Samuel 17:33, Saul was telling David that he couldn't fight Goliath because he was too young and wasn't even a man of war. By verse 51, David was standing over Goliath's lifeless body, using Goliath's own sword to cut off his head!

In Nehemiah 4:3, the opposition said that "if a fox go up, he shall even break down their stone wall." Nehemiah 6:15 reads,

> So the wall was finished in the twenty and fifth day of the month Elul, in fifty and two days.

I made it through a couple of examples trying to be as brief and to the point as possible. To fully strengthen my point, I want to look over the life of someone whom we can relate to more and can clearly see his failures that come before his success. We can clearly see how much patience and effort must be put into becoming someone, changing who we used to be and overcoming our old ways.

If you were assembling a team or a group of men to do something incredible, wouldn't you want to choose well-developed and respected men? From what I've read, none of the other first twelve apostles had the struggles that Peter had. Jesus often took Peter, James, and John off to pray alone. But Peter separated himself from the rest of the apostles by what he did while on this new journey through life. John 1:42 reads,

> And he brought him to Jesus. And when Jesus beheld him, he said, Thou art Simon the son of Jona: thou shalt be called Cephas, which is by interpretation, A stone.

At this time, Peter was far from a stone. Think about the word *stone* or *rock*. It's solid. Stones are used to build structures that are made to be very stable. Peter was far from stable at this time, but when someone decides to become a doctor, do they just instantly become one? Or does it take years and years of time and effort?

Don't Give Up

One of the first things that Peter said to Jesus is to leave him alone because he didn't feel worthy. Luke 5:8 reads,

> When Simon Peter saw it, he fell down at Jesus' knees, saying, Depart from me; for I am a sinful man, O Lord.

Peter's past meant nothing to Jesus. In verse 10, Jesus spoke these words:

> Fear not; from henceforth thou shalt catch men.

When this took place, Peter was simply fishing for fish. Jesus then told Peter he was much more than just a fisherman. Jesus told him that now he would fish for people. Meaning, he would now help lead people to God through Jesus Christ. I believe I can accurately say Peter tried harder than the rest of the apostles. I suppose some may have simply understood things quicker or easier than him, but

Peter's misunderstandings didn't come from a lack of effort or desire. That's all God really wants from us: for us to put forth the effort.

The next example I want to give you is another time when Peter tried something incredible, but all he ended up doing was "getting it wrong." Matthew 4:25–32 is the story of Jesus walking on water, but let's examine the conversation and actions between Peter and Jesus.

> *Jesus said*, "Be of good cheer; it is I; be not afraid."
>
> *Peter said*, "Lord, if it be thou, bid me come unto thee on the water."
>
> *Jesus said*, "Come."

Matthew 29–32 reads,

> And he said, Come. And when Peter was come down out of the ship, he walked on the water, to go to Jesus. But when he saw the wind boisterous, he was afraid; and beginning to sink, he cried, saying, Lord, save me. And immediately Jesus stretched forth his hand, and caught him, and said unto him, O thou of little faith, wherefore didst thou doubt. And when they were come into the ship, the wind ceased.

Can you imagine how Peter felt the second he was sitting safely in the boat again just after the wind had stopped, just after hearing the words of Jesus, "O thou of little faith, wherefore didst thou doubt"? But also consider this: Peter was the only one to get out on the water and try.

Let's now look at a conversation between Jesus and Peter in Matthew 13–23. Jesus asked his disciples who men say that he is. It then says that *they* said that some said he was John the Baptist, some said Elijah, and others said Jeremiah or one of the prophets. He asked them who they say he is.

> *Peter said,* "Thou are the Christ, the Son of the living God."

> *Jesus said,* "Blessed art thou, Simon Bar-jona: for flesh and blood hath not revealed it unto thee, but my Father which is in heaven. And I say also unto thee, That thou art Peter, and upon this rock I will build my church; and the gates of hell shall not prevail against it. And I will give unto thee the keys of the kingdom of heaven: and whatsoever thou shalt bind on earth shall be bound in heaven: and whatsoever thou shalt loose on earth shall be loosed in heaven."

Jesus then began to show his disciples that he must suffer and be killed and raised on the third day, and then this happened:

> *Peter said,* "Be it far from thee, Lord: this shall not be unto thee."

Now look at verse 23:

> *Jesus said,* "Get thee behind me, Satan: thou art an offence unto me: for thou savourest not the things that be of God, but those that be of men."

This is almost like the walking-on-water incident all over again. Peter answered his question and then got one of the biggest compliments in the world, being told Jesus would use him to build his church. Just as Peter did, in fact, step out onto the water and begin walking on water, doing something incredible—just as he "stepped out on the water" by answering a question that could have easily ended with a very negative response—he began to sink, and Jesus had to look at him and tell him he did something wrong by doubting. In the same manner, just as fast as Peter gave a correct answer and got a huge compliment, not but a couple moments later, he was being called Satan.

Have you ever been in a class, or possibly just in a group with other humans, and someone was explaining something you didn't understand? But since others were showing that they did, you simply pretended to understand because you didn't want anyone to know that you really didn't? I believe this is something most of us have done a time or two and something that some people probably do too often. One of the things I like most about Peter is he was never afraid to ask questions. Some of the rest of the apostles seemed to be able to just sit back and learn without asking questions (or at least they weren't documented), or perhaps some of them had the same questions as Peter but didn't want to be the ones to come forward and admit they didn't understand. Peter is a perfect example of why you can't be afraid to ask questions. Here are a few questions Peter asked.

> Lord, how oft shall my brother sin against me, and I forgive him? (Matthew 18:21)

> Behold, we have forsaken all, and followed thee; what shall we have therefore? (Matthew 19:27)

> Speakest thou this parable unto us, or even to all? (Luke 12:41)

> Lord, and what shall this man do? (John 21:21)

Matthew 26:33–35 reads,

> Peter answered and said unto him, Though all men shall be offended because of thee, yet will I never be offended Jesus said unto him, Verily I say unto thee, That this night, before the cock crow, thou shalt deny thrice. Peter said unto him, Though I should die with thee, yet will I not deny thee. Likewise also said all the disciples.

Between the verses of Matthew 26:66 to 74, Peter denied Jesus three times, but I'm only going to include verse 74:

> Then he began to curse and to swear, saying, I know not the man. And immediately the cock crew.

It then says Peter remembered Jesus's words and went out and wept bitterly. Peter did many other things that show that he was far from perfect, such as falling asleep after Jesus told him to watch with him and got this response in Matthew 26:40:

> And he cometh unto the disciples and findeth them asleep and said unto Peter, What could ye not watch with me one hour?

Peter also cut off the ear of Malchus, thinking he was doing the right thing by standing up for Jesus; but Jesus healed the man's ear, showing that, once again, Peter was wrong. But after all of Peter's, in the book of Acts, we clearly see that Peter finally got it right. Simon Peter is a great example of what can happen to someone who actually tries. If you removed the names, you'd hardly recognize the Peter we see in the book of Acts from the Peter we read about in the Gospels. Over and over in the book of Acts, you see that Peter stood up and spoke to crowds and corrected the mistakes and misinterpretations of others. To finish making my point, I'm going to pull a few verses out of the two epistles he wrote.

> Seeing ye have purified your souls in obeying the truth through the Spirit unto unfeigned love of the brethren, see that ye love one another with a pure heart fervently: being born again, not of corruptible seed, but of incorruptible, by the word of God, which liveth and abideth for ever. (1 Peter 1:22–23)

> But ye are a chosen generation, a royal priesthood, an holy nation, a peculiar people; that ye should shew forth the praises of him who hath called you out of darkness into his marvelous light. (1 Peter 2: 9)

> Let him eschew evil, and do good; let him seek peace, and ensue it. (1 Peter 3:11)

> But sanctify the Lord God in your hearts: and be ready always to give an answer to every man

that asketh you a reason of the hope that is in you with meakness and fear. (1 Peter 3:15)

For if God spared not the angels that sinned, but cast down to hell, and delivered them into chains of darkness, to be reserved unto judgment; and spared not the old world, but saved Noah the eighth person, a preacher of righteousness, bringing in the flood upon the world of the ungodly; and turning the cities of Sodom and Gomorrha into ashes condemned them with an overthrow making them an ensample unto those that after should live ungodly; and delivered just Lot, vexed with the filthy conversation of the wicked: (for that righteous man dwelling among them, in seeing and hearing, vexed his righteous soul from day to day with their unlawful deeds;) the Lord knoweth how to deliver the godly out of temptation, and to reserve the unjust unto the day of judgment to be punished. (2 Peter 4–9)

I'm about to stress one thing that is very important. Peter didn't learn everything from simply being with Jesus and listening to him speak; he learned from the same scriptures we have available to us. You should have noticed him mentioning several of the men I've already covered in this book. Acts 1:20 contains the words being spoken by Peter, saying, "For it is written in the book of Psalms." If you read 1 Peter 3:11 and Psalms 34:14, you will clearly see where Peter got that words he used in his own epistle. Remember, Jesus stood up and read from the book of Isaiah. Does this help show you the importance of reading the Bible for yourself? Remember, I said you'd hardly recognize Peter without seeing his name; this is the new Peter you can read about in the book of Acts.

- Peter stood up in the midst of the disciples and said they needed to fulfill the scriptures by choosing Judas Iscariot's replacement (Acts 1:15–26).
- Peter stood up and addressed the people, correcting them on a false assumption by saying that the words spoken by the prophet Joel were simply being fulfilled (Acts 2:14–16).
- Then Peter said to them, "Repent, and let every one of you be baptized in the name of Jesus Christ for the remission of sins; and you shall receive the gift of the Holy Spirit"(Acts 2:38).
- Then Peter said, "Silver and gold I do not have, but what I do have I give you: In the name of Jesus Christ of Nazareth, rise up and walk" (Acts 3:6).
- So when Peter saw it, he responded to the people, "Men of Israel, why do you marvel at this? Or why look so intently at us, as though by our own power or godliness we had made this man walk?"
- "Now when they saw the boldness of Peter and John, and perceived that they were uneducated and untrained, they marveled. And they realized that they had been with Jesus" (Acts 4:13).

These are just a few verses that show an obvious change from the man who didn't seem to be able to do anything right while right beside Jesus. Another great response Peter gave comes in Acts 4:19, just after being told they couldn't speak in the name of Jesus. Peter and John replied,

> Whether it is right in the sight of God to listen to you more than God, you Judge.

Perhaps this hasn't impressed you, so maybe I should tell you of a time when Peter was the one being sent for to raise a woman from the dead, the time when an angel was sent to rescue him from prison, or the time when he called a couple out on why they thought they could lie to the Holy Spirit, for which, in return, they both dropped dead. But I'll finish displaying the progress of Peter with this story of how he was the man to clear up a very big dispute on the truth behind circumcision.

Acts 10:9 begins with Peter going up to pray and having a vision in which he saw some unclean animals and heard the Lord tell him to rise up and eat. But Peter refused, saying he had never eaten anything that was common or unclean. But the voice replied, "What God has cleansed you must not call common." Peter didn't understand it at first, but three men were being sent to him, men whom he had previously had been taught not to associate with; but when they arrived, he understood. Acts 10:34 reads,

> Then Peter opened his mouth, and said, Of a truth I perceive that God is no respecter of persons: but in every nation that heareth him, and worketh righteousness, is accepted with him.

Acts 15:1 reads,

> And certain men which came down from Judaea taught the brethren, and said, Except ye be circumcised after the manner of Moses, ye cannot be saved.

Paul and Barnabas disagreed, so they decided to go talk to the elders and apostles, during which the man to stand up and settle the dispute was the once-uncertain Peter. Acts 15:7–9 reads,

> And when there had been much disputing, Peter rose up, and said unto them, Men and brethren, ye know how that a good while ago God made a choice among us, that the Gentiles by my mouth should hear the word of the gospel and believe. And God, which knoweth the hearts, bare them witness, giving them the Holy Ghost, even as he did unto us; and put no difference between us and them, purifying their hearts by faith.

If you haven't noticed, the man who fell down to his knees and told Jesus to depart from him because he was a sinner had now become a bold and confident man of God. In the Gospels, James, Peter, and John were pulled aside on several occasions. John wrote five books, but John wrote about one thing in particular more than anything. He wrote about *love*.

Chapter 14

THE GREATEST OF THESE

Three things will last forever—faith, hope, and love—and the greatest of these is love.

This verse is taken from 1 Corinthians 13:13. Love has always been hard for me to understand; for some reason, I always feel love meant more to me than most people. Love seems to be thrown around meaninglessly. It seems to me that, to most people, *love* is nothing more than a word. Just another meaningless word!

Before we get into what love is, let's talk about the other two for just a moment. First of all, what is hope? Well, hope is simply a thought. You can be hoping for something, and no one would ever know it. So what is joy? Joy is a feeling. It is much easier to tell when someone has joy because they usually express it. Joy could be expressed in many different ways, in the form of anything from smiling, to dancing, singing, screaming loudly, etc. The NLT version of the Bible words Proverbs 13:12 this way:

> Hope deferred makes the heart sick, but when
> dreams come true, there is life and joy.

What I just heard was that a thought has the ability to control a feeling. So if hope is a thought and joy is a feeling, what is love? From watching the rest of the world and how they use it, I'd have to say that love is nothing but a word, a word you use to manipulate people. Before I tell you what I believe love is, let me teach you a few things about the word *love*.

The Ancient Greeks actually use four different terms to symbolize the four types of love. We have *eros, storge, agape,* and *phileo*. Eros love is said to be a romantic love. Storge is more of the love you have for your family. Phileo love is a brotherly love among friends. And agape love is an unconditional love, the kind of love God has for us.

I believe this is the key to happiness. If you're human, you probably want and/or need to have each of these four types of love present in your life, but unfortunately, most of us can't seem to get them all in our lives at the same time. I'm going to try and help explain how and why this is possible and why it's not very common. The first type of love we have in our lives is agape, but agape love is something that people can go through their whole lives and never truly feel.

Storge love. This is the first kind of love that we'll truly experience. When I look back to my earliest memories, they always involve family. Remember how Joseph's brothers felt about him? They didn't exactly show that they loved him when they sold him into slavery. Now look at how Joseph felt toward them. He forgave them when they horribly wronged him and then allowed his family to move to Egypt where he had worked his way to the top. Joseph allowed them to share in his success, even after they had horribly wronged him. Joseph displayed the way you should feel toward your family. He displayed how you should act when you love someone. He could have stayed bitter and sent them away with nothing, knowing that they'd starve to death, and he'd have his revenge, but that isn't what love is.

One of the best examples of what family is really about is found in the book of Ruth. The book of Ruth begins with three women—three widows, to be more specific. One was named Naomi, who had two daughters-in-law: Orpah and Ruth. After her sons died, she displayed the fact that she truly loved her daughters-in-law and only wanted them to be happy. She told them both to leave and go back to their own mothers' home and to marry again because they were young enough that they still had their whole lives ahead of them. That's what love should really be about: simply wanting what is best for them, not yourself, and wanting them to be happy, even if it means you are in a worse situation.

That doesn't mean one family member accepts anything offered and never cares what situation the other is left in. Orpah didn't necessarily do anything wrong. Her husband died; that wasn't her choice. She deserved to move on and be happy, but what Ruth does is beyond simply right or wrong. What Ruth does is so incredible it earned her the entire eighth book of the Bible.

Ruth refused to leave her mother-in-law. Are you aware of how many movies have been made regarding in-laws with the main point being that they hate each other? Ruth told Naomi she would not leave her and ended up staying with her and working in the field to support herself and her mother-in-law. Naomi never asked her family to put themselves in a worse spot for her benefit, and Ruth wouldn't pursue her own happiness if it meant putting her family in a worse situation. I believe that true family love was displayed in that story.

> A friend is always loyal, and a brother is born to
> help in the time of need. (Proverbs 17:17)

Phileo love. Isn't it amazing how little family really matters once you begin to make friends, or at least people we call friends? I believe the most well-known friendship is going to be that of the relationship between David and Jonathan. Second Samuel 1:26 reads,

> I am distressed for thee, my brother Jonathan: very pleasant hast thou been unto me: thy love to me was wonderful, passing the love of women.

Jonathan went against his own father to protect his friendship with David and stay loyal. So how did other friends in the Bible handle their friendship role?

In the book of Daniel, we see how friends stuck together no matter what the cost, even if it meant being thrown in a fiery furnace together. In the book of Job, we see friends traveling to be with a friend who was going through terrible times. When you have a real friend, they begin to be more like family than simply a friend. The type of love you have for these types of people in your life should grow over time.

> Two are better than one; because they have a good reward for their labour. For if they fall, the one will lift up his fellow: but woe to him that is alone when he falleth; for he hath not another to help him up. Again, if two lie together, then they have heat: but how can one be warm alone? And if one prevail against him, two shall withstand him; and a threefold cord is not quickly broken. (Ecclesiastes 4:9)

Eros love. Of all the love among humans, perhaps this is the most important one of them all. Here is why I can say that with confidence. Genesis 2:24 reads,

> Therefore shall a man leave his father and his mother, and shall cleave unto his wife: and they shall be one flesh.

This is so important because in this type of love, the two parties are actually one. This means that no matter what either does, both should be affected the same. In the other types of love, it's very common for both parties to be affected completely differently.

Here is the problem with my theory, though. Unfortunately, that's not how it is always. In so many instances, marriages end when only one of the two are doing something wrong. When that happens, there also comes proof that my theory may also possibly be correct.

When two people join for marriage, they are telling each other that, for the rest of their lives, they will love each other no matter what. This means that if one side separates from the other, it could leave the other in a worse place than before they were married.

Have you ever tried to pull apart an Oreo? Have you ever tried to pull one apart and have both sides look exactly the same and each be 50 percent of the cookie? Meaning, you could pull apart two Oreos and then use one piece from one Oreo and put it together with the piece from the other Oreo and have it fit perfectly, looking like those were the original two sides to the cookie.

I'm not saying that you can't get divorced and then remarry and be just as happy as before or happier, but consider this. If you still deeply love someone who is divorcing you, you're not going to be completely happy with anyone else. And if you are happier with your new spouse than you ever were with your previous, doesn't that kind of say that you married the wrong person the first time? This could possibly be indicating you jumped into marriage without first testing whether or not they were the right person for you.

If you're on the same page as me, you realize that phileo and storge love are the most similar. Once you have eros love in your life, you should be able to endure significant lengths of time without seeing your friends and family without it constantly affecting your ability to function properly in life. But think about this: if the person you're in love with stayed out all night for just one whole night without proper communication, wouldn't that really bother you? And if you can go a significant length of time without seeing them, what does that say about how you feel about them?

Agape love. This is perhaps the most powerful love. It is a love that moves, and when it moves, it moves in two directions. The first direction agape love has to go is vertical. This love is between you and God; but once this love is established, it must go horizontal, which means it is now between you and the other people living among you in this world.

I read a book that described it like this: If you only have the vertical love and not the horizontal (meaning, you have no one to share it with or are just refusing to share it), it will be like a birdbath that fills up and, when it is full, just begins to overflow and spill out haphazardly. I've actually experienced this and can verify its truth.

The more you love God, the more you will want to show your love for others. And when you truly love God, it won't matter if someone is a friend or your blood family. Your love will be for all people and will be shown whenever someone is in need.

Jesus said in Matthew 12:50, "For whosoever shall do the will of my Father which is in heaven, the same is my brother, and sister, and mother." But also remember that Jesus healed those who weren't just his "brother, sister, or mother," which, in our world, translates to family. Jesus healing anyone shows that he truly had unconditional love for us, not just his friends and family. That's what agape is. When you can take your time and money to help people you don't know and have never met simply because they need it, that says your love comes from God. It says that your love is *agape*.

I used to hear all the time that you have to be friends with someone before you are in a real relationship with them. I always thought this was absurd. That's not exactly true, but I do understand why they say that now. It all made sense after I learned about these different types of love.

What I've noticed about unhappy relationships or marriages is it often comes from either the man or woman choosing their time with friends over the responsibility they signed up for with marriage, or stepping into that commitment that leads to marriage. If you don't get that friendship love from your significant other and children, you are going to either be unhappy or pursue it, which cuts into your children and significant other's time with you and their happiness.

Another reason for unhappiness is the lack of agape love from God. We have free will, which is the ability to make our own decisions. That doesn't mean that God doesn't have a plan for us, a plan that he has because he loves us. If you haven't accepted that love, the love we receive through God's Son, Jesus Christ, you'll never understand God's plan for you. That alone may very well result in your unhappiness. I read that one of the biggest reasons for unhappiness is simply not living out God's plan for your life. The Bible says resist the devil, but if you're resisting God, you're resisting agape love. This means you're missing a portion of the love you need to have complete happiness.

> Love is patient and kind. Love is not jealous or boastful or proud or rude. Love does not demand its own way. Love is not irritable, and it keeps no record of when it has been wronged. It is never glad about injustice but rejoices

> when the truth wins out. Love never gives up, never loses faith, is always hopeful and endures through every circumstance. Love will last forever, but prophecy and speaking in unknown languages and special knowledge will all disappear. (1 Corinthians 13:4–8)
>
> But anyone who does not love does not know God—for God is love. (1 John 4:8)

The closer I get to God, the more I think about how to spread God's love to others. As I began to think about how to do it in the most appropriate and efficient manner, I had to first consider a few things. In the beginning, the earth was filled with darkness until Genesis 1:3, when God said, "Let there be light," and there was light. We now consider light to be good and darkness to be evil. We consider love to be good and hate to be evil. So if what I just said is all true, then *darkness*, *evil*, and *hate* are all synonymous; meaning *light*, *good*, and *love* are all synonymous.

> Let your light so shine before men, that they may see your good works, and glorify your Father which is in heaven. (Matthew 5:16)
>
> For it is God which worketh in you both to will and to do of his good pleasure. (Philippians 2:13)
>
> Love worketh no ill to his neighbor: therefore love is the fulfilling of the law. (Romans 13:10)

So when I put these three verses together, what I hear is that to bring light into this world, we do it by doing good works, which come from God working within us, and we should never have to think twice about doing something if we are doing it out of love.

Chapter 15

A Ticket Home

Picture this: there was a man who was in America simply visiting from a foreign country. He couldn't speak a word of English. His family helped him get his ticket paid for and left him at the airport, where he was to just wait for his plane and get back to his homeland.

Just a little while before the man's flight, he reached into his pocket and noticed that he no longer had his ticket. He began to panic. He looked around a little bit and even tried to ask a few Americans, who couldn't help him because they had no way to communicate properly.

After just a few minutes of searching desperately, the man realized it could be anywhere; and if he were to look for it over the whole airport, he would never make his flight anyway. The man returned to his seat and sat quietly, not really knowing what to do and feeling as if he may never make it home.

To his surprise, a young gentleman came up to him and gently tapped him on the shoulder to get his attention. When the man looked at him, much to his surprise, he was holding out the ticket he thought he had lost. Knowing they spoke different languages, the man simply nodded with a smile and took his ticket. The young man walked away just as calmly as he came.

The point of this story is that it took no words for the man to realize whom the ticket belonged simply because it was obvious the man belonged to the place where the ticket was headed to. It wasn't a very common country, there weren't many people getting on that plane, and there was no one else in that area who could claim that ticket. By simply looking at the man, the young man knew he was the one going to that particular location.

Jesus Explains

Wouldn't it be nice if someone you'd never seen before was handing out tickets to heaven, and they just walked up and handed you one? And when you saw where the ticket was to, you could confidently reach out and grab it, knowing it was yours? Matthew 13: 24–30 reads,

> Another parable put he forth unto them, saying, The kingdom of heaven is likened unto a man which sowed good seed in his field: but while men slept, his enemy came and sowed tares among the wheat, and went his way. But when the blade was sprung up, and brought forth fruit, then appeared the tares also. So the servants of the householder came and said unto him, Sir, didst not thou sow good seed in thy field? From whence then hath it tares? He said unto them, An enemy hath done this. The servants said unto him, Wilt thou then that we go and gather them up? But he said, Nay; lest while ye gather up the tares, ye root up also the wheat with them. Let both grow together until

> the harvest: and in the time of the harvest I will say to the reapers, Gather ye together first the tares, and bind them in bundles to burn them: but gather the wheat into my barn.

His disciples then asked him what this parable meant, and this is what Jesus replied, starting at verse 37:

> He answered and said unto them, He that soweth the good seed is the Son of man; the field is the world; the good seed are the children of the kingdom; but the tares are the children of the wicked one; the enemy that sowed them is the devil; the harvest is the end of the world; and the reapers are the angels. As therefore the tares are gathered and burned in the fire; so shall it be in the end of the world. The Son of man shall send forth his angels, and they shall gather out of his kingdom all the things that offend, and them which do iniquity; and shall cast them into a furnace of fire there shall be wailing and gnashing as teeth. Then shall the righteous shine forth as the sun in the kingdom of their father. Who hath ears to hear; let him hear.

Too Close for Comfort

One time, I was asked to cut some weeds out of a plant bed; and let me tell you, it was very frustrating trying to make sure not to cut out any of the good ones because some were so close to death and looked like weeds.

When those angels come back to gather the "tares" to be burned, I don't want to be mistaken for one. Luke 6:44 tells us that a tree is known by its fruit. The previous verse tells us that a good tree can only bring forth good fruit and a corrupt tree can't bring forth good fruit. If you walked up to an apple tree that was full of fresh apples, you'd have no doubts that it was, in fact, an apple tree. The same thing could be said for a peach, plum, cherry, etc. But what if there was no fruit on any of them? Would you have the confidence to accurately name every tree that had no fruit on them? It's time we start producing good fruit. It's time we separate ourselves as wheat among the tares. It's time we become someone who can be handed our ticket to heaven without having to tell someone that, that is where we are headed.

Think About It

The title of this chapter is "A Ticket Home," with the assumption that everyone would like to be handed that "ticket to heaven." But here is the unfortunate truth of the matter. If you asked someone if they'd rather be rich or poor, what do you think they'd say? I'm guessing rich. If you asked someone if they'd rather go to heaven or hell, what do you think they'd say? I'm guessing heaven. So if you're being honest, you probably just said that people want to be rich and go to heaven. Listen to what Jesus said in Matthew 20:23–24:

> Then said Jesus unto his disciples, Verily I say unto you, That a rich man shall hardly enter into the kingdom of heaven. And again I say unto you, It is easier for a camel to go through the eye of a needle, than for a rich man to enter the kingdom of God.

So if you heard what I just heard, people unknowingly are saying that they don't mind having only a small chance at getting to heaven. Just before he made that statement, a rich young man came to Jesus and asked him what he had to do to get to heaven, and Jesus told him to go sell all he had and give to the poor. So Jesus basically gave him an option. You can be rich here on earth, or you can have everlasting life in heaven. Chapter 19 verse 22 tells us that the man chose to stay rich on earth.

> But when the young man heard that saying, he went away sorrowful: for he had great possessions.

It appears to me that every day, people are making that same decision, whether they know it or not. I'd like to think that most kids growing up have dreams of being rich. They talk about buying their mommy a big house with a swimming pool, giving to the poor, etc. But it appears to me what they don't do is *account for variable change*. Lots of things can be said about money, but one thing, which is a well-known saying, that fits perfectly to the point I'm trying to make is, "Money changes people." Look at King Solomon, the wisest king ever. God came to him and told him he could ask for anything. First Kings 3:9 reads,

> Give therefore thy servant an understanding heart to judge thy people, that I may discern between good and bad: for who is able to judge this thy so great a people?

God then basically, in verses 10–13, says since Solomon's was thinking about the right things and didn't ask for a long life or for the death of his enemies, he would grant his request. But, also, God added riches. Now, if you look to the book of Ecclesiastes, a book written by Solomon, you see that he tried to buy his happiness. If you read the book of Ecclesiastes, it's more than clear that Solomon was far from happy. It's also more than clear that Solomon's thoughts changed some time after he gained wealth.

After I started writing this book, I asked someone, "If you could ask God anything, what would it be?" They said, "Am I coming to heaven?" Although that's a very reasonable response, and something I'm sure almost anyone who truly believes in God would like to know, the answer is very simple: It's your decision. It's decided by your choices and actions.

In Luke 15:11–32, there's a story of a man who had two sons, and one son asked for his portion of his inheritance and leaves; but when he ran out of money, he began to work for someone else. He then decided that he'd rather be working for his father than anyone else, so he decided to go back home. Actually, he chose to go back home. His father never told him to leave; he chose to leave. But when he returned, his father saw him coming in the distance and ran out to meet him. The father then clothed him with the best robe, put a ring on his hand and sandals on his feet, and prepared a fatted calf. Luke 15:24 reads,

> For this my son was dead, and is alive again; he was lost, and is found. And they began to be merry.

Now, let me ask you a question. What is something that could have kept the son from returning to his father? If you said pride, you'd be correct. Pride has been one of the biggest downfalls of men since the beginning of time. Satan used to lead worship in heaven as an angel, but his pride caused his fall. King after king has been removed from his throne due to his pride. Sometimes simply humbling yourself enough to admit you were wrong is all it takes to change your life.

Romans 10:13 says, "For whosoever shall call upon the name of the Lord shall be saved." It appears to me that the matter of getting to heaven or not is simply a matter of if we choose to. Don't let that be misunderstood that by getting to heaven is a matter of saying we are or we aren't. There are many choices we'll have to make that aren't as simple as talking. Within simply saying we want to go to heaven, there will then be trials and tribulations that face us with "choices," which will ultimately decide whether we are handed that ticket to heaven or not.

Getting that ticket to heaven isn't even close to impossible as you just heard Paul say that anyone can do it. However, you have to be 100 percent sincere when you call upon the name of the Lord, or you may get the impression God didn't hear you.

Check Your Insides First

Remember the story of the boy who cried wolf. He falsely cried wolf many times; then when the wolf was really there, nobody listened. The good thing about God is that he always listens. Some people will tell you that all you have to do to be saved is say a simple prayer. I had people tell me all I had to do was say this prayer, and I'd be saved. I said this prayer several times, and never did I feel anything. I can confidently say nothing changed.

After at least four years from the time I said this prayer for the last time, I was finally saved. Using that information, what I believe the secret to truly being saved is simply that circumcision of the heart that Paul talked about. There are countless evils you may have to remove from your heart before you are truly saved, but I'm only going to talk about a couple of the main ones that will definitely keep you from getting that ticket home. What I've noticed are three main things that could keep someone out of heaven: unforgiveness, pride, and the love of money (greed).

Jesus teaches us about forgiveness with a very simple and meaningful parable in Matthew 18:21–35. Jesus began by saying that the kingdom of heaven is like a king who had a servant who owed him more than he could pay. The servant fell down and asked for more time to pay the debt. Matthew 18:27 reads,

> Then the lord of that servant was moved with compassion, and loosed him, and forgave him the debt.

Now this same servant who was just forgiven was owed by someone else and did not show the same compassion his master showed him. Matthew 18:28–30 reads,

> But the same servant went out, and found one of his fellowservants, which owed him an hundred pence: and he laid hands on him, and took him by the throat saying, Pay me that thou owest. And his fellowservant fell down at this feet, and besought him, saying, Have patience with me and I will pay thee all. And he would not: but went and cast him into prison, till he should pay the debt.

After finding out that the servant whom he forgave failed to show the same forgiveness to his fellow servant, this is how their master reacted. Matthew 18:34–35 reads,

> And his lord was wroth, and delivered him to the tormentors, till he should pay all that was due

> unto hm. So likewise shall my heavenly Father
> do also unto you, if ye from your hearts forgive
> not every one his brother their trespasses.

Jesus gave this parable after Peter asked a very good question. He asked how many times we are to forgive someone who wrongs us. At the times I said the prayer that is supposed to save you, I had a different mentality than I did when I was truly saved. I felt I was too forgiving; I had this mentality where I'd forgive someone uncontrollably. I had to fight my own thoughts to remind myself how bad they wronged me and that I shouldn't have forgiven them. I told myself they didn't deserve to be forgiven. I can clearly see the first part of Matthew 18:35—"so likewise shall my heavenly Father do also unto you"—being inserted into my life at the times I prayed the prayer, which is why God wasn't willing to grant my salvation.

I had someone ask me a question about pride or, more specifically, being proud. After hearing the verse that tells us that God resists the proud but gives grace to the humble, they asked me if we aren't supposed to be proud of things we do, such as something we accomplished with our work. A long time ago, I learned of the term *false pride*. Genesis 1:31 reads,

> And God saw everything that he had made,
> and, behold, it was very good.

God just displayed what I call pride. Genesis 18:16–33 is the story of when God decided to destroy Sodom and Gomorrah for their wickedness. Abraham interceded and asked God if he'd destroy all the men even if some were righteous. Pride could have kept God from sparing the life of Lot. Also, the same thing happened when God wanted to kill all the Israelites for worshiping a golden calf. Moses reminded God of his promise, and God changed his mind. In the parable of the lost son, the younger son wouldn't have had the ability to admit he was wrong and would have never tried to go back home if he was filled with pride.

Can I Get a Definition Check?

The problems with words these days are there are so many definitions for what they are, nobody really knows the true definition anymore. If you showed me a football, I'd say it's a football and there is no other name I'd call it. If you showed me a soccer ball I'd call it a soccer ball and there is no other name I'd call it. But if we were in England and you showed me a soccer ball, I'd call it a football.

If a woman saw that her son had all A's on his report card, you'd say she felt "proud" of her son, right? So is this wrong? Well, in Matthew 3:17, God looked down and said, "This is my beloved Son, in whom I am well pleased." It never says that God was "proud" of his Son, but *pride* is the word we associate with that feeling of being pleased with something. The term I've heard associated with Satan is *pride*.

If you read Ezekiel 28, it describes Satan. Nowhere in my Bible does it say the word *pride*. It's a description that some humans have labeled "pride." So what I'm saying is, don't get too caught up in thinking that the word *pride* itself is what will keep us from heaven, or that it's displeasing to God—it's the result from it. Remember, humility pleases God. For me, the times when I'm most humble are the times when I begin to feel overly proud. I believe it's sort of an insecurity issue. If I'm so "proud" of something, I feel it's the best; there is no insecurity, and no feeling of needing to tell others how good I did to prove myself.

I've noticed at times that if I don't feel that initial "pride," then sometimes I forget to be humble. I believe with all my heart that you can be "proud" of being "humble." I believe that *pride* is a word. The thing that God resists is a behavior or action. Actually, when I read the description of Satan in Ezekiel, I think that the words *arrogance* or *conceit* fit much better than *pride*. In fact, I believe Satan should have been "proud" to worship God. I'm about to give you some definitions of pride that come from my dictionary app:

1. A sense of one's own proper dignity or value; self-respect
2. Pleasure or satisfaction taken in an achievement, possession, or association
3. Arrogant or disdainful conduct or treatment; haughtiness
4. An excessively high opinion of oneself; conceit

Notice that the first one doesn't sound bad at all. With the second one, you can see small warning signs. But the last two are very different from the first definition. So why do we have so many definitions for one word? That's a question I can't answer, but all I know is it leaves people who read the Bible or hear that having pride is a bad thing questioning themselves and wondering what is right.

We earlier saw the story of the man who asked Jesus what he would have to do to get to heaven and walked away sorrowfully when Jesus told him that he would have to sell everything he had and give to the poor. Having money wasn't what was keeping the man from getting to heaven; it was his love for money, choosing money over God.

When new players enter the NFL, they go through training camps and such, and one thing they do for rookies is have a former NFL player come in and talk to them about life. They try to prepare them for the lifestyle changes that are ahead that come with money and fame. A better example may be the people who get rich because they are too cheap to spend their money. They will hardly spend it on themselves, let alone anyone else.

Overcoming Satan

Before you get an opportunity to use the ticket you have already received, the devil is going to do anything he can to make sure you lose it. There is only one way you can hold on to that ticket. James 4:7 reads,

> Submit yourselves therefore to God. Resist the devil, and he will flee from you.

Now you know how to beat the devil—plain and simple, right? So where did James get this piece of wisdom from? Why didn't Jesus say this? Think about this for just a second. If the devil hadn't deceived humans, there would be no sin. If Satan wasn't on earth or was helpless, how different would this world be? So we have this incredible Bible verse, but why does James make this seem so simple, and where did he get this from?

I looked in Proverbs, I looked in the gospels, and nowhere did I find those words from anyone else. But open with me to the book of Luke. Luke 4: 13 reads,

> And when the devil had ended all the temptation, he departed from him for a season.

So how did he get the devil to depart from him? He did exactly what James wrote: he resisted him.

At some point everything's going to go south on you, everything's going to go south and you're going to say this is it, this is how I end. Now you can either accept that or you can get to work, that's all it is, you just, you do the math, you solve one problem and then you solve the next one and then the next, and if you solve enough of them, you get to come home.
—Matt Damon, *The Martian*

Chapter 16

The Formula

When I was first asked where to start when reading the Bible, I wasn't really sure what to say. I was asked this question by someone, and at the time, I told them to read Psalms because that's what I did. The psalms are easy to read, easy to understand, and very encouraging and comforting. But now, after I have become what I call someone who is able to read the Bible efficiently and understand it, I believe I can answer that question much easier and with a lot more confidence.

I don't remember this being in the moment, but I have old home videos of me learning to ride a bike. I was obviously excited to get on the bike and learn to ride with no training wheels. I was very willing to ride at the start of the video. But as time went on, after failing and falling and seeming to make no progress, I began to get frustrated; and after getting hurt and crying, I wanted to quit. Now I have no memory of actually learning to ride the bike, but I know that, to this day, I can get on a bike and ride it with no problems. I do have memories of being younger riding a bike with my friends and smiling and having the time of my life. The point I'm trying to make is, most things are more fun once you're actually good at them or able to do them. I know a lot of people who enjoy bowling, and a lot of those people aren't good at it; most get an average of 80–100. Now,

I'd be willing to bet someone who threw a gutter ball every single attempt would never make it to, let's just say, a fiftieth game, which I'm guessing everyone I've bowled with and was referring to in my previous statement had bowled at least that many games. You have to see some sort of progress, or at least feel you're doing something for it to be worth continuing. So my first tip for reading the Bible on your own is learn a few facts, such as the following:

1. There are sixty-six books in the Holy Bible (seventy-three in the Catholic Bible), thirty-nine in the Old Testament and twenty-seven in the New Testament.
2. There are 150 psalms, which make up the longest book in the Bible.
3. There are thirty-one proverbs (lots of people read one chapter a day to read the book of Proverbs every month).

Now I'm going to teach you one of the first things I ever learned about the Bible that has stuck with me for ten years. If I asked you some questions concerning the story in which Peter cut off the ear of a high priest's servant, a story that is in all four Gospels—if I asked these questions: (1) Who cut off the ear of the high priest's servant? (2) What was the name of the high priest's servant whose ear was cut off? (3) Which ear of the high priest's servant was cut off? (4) What did Jesus do after the high priest's servant's ear was cut off?—you could not accurately answer those four simple questions without reading all four of the Gospels. You can read it for yourself in Matthew 26:51, Mark 14:47, Luke 22:50, and John 18:10. But if you notice, Matthew does not tell you which disciple cut off the ear, which ear it was, what the name of the servant was, or what Jesus did with the ear. Mark tells us just about the same information. Now, if you read Luke, you'll finally get the answer to numbers 3 and 4, that it was the right ear and that Jesus healed the high priest's servant's ear.

Then, in John, you finally get the name of the disciple and the name of the high priest's servant, which is Malchus.

Another small fact I learned very early in my isolated Bible reading was the size of the ark built by Noah. The ark was 450 feet long, 75 feet wide, and 45 feet tall. The King James Version will tell you that the length was 300 cubits, the breadth was 50 cubits, and the height was 30 cubits. So what I had to learn, first of all, was what a cubit was. A cubit is 18 inches. I also didn't know what breadth was but quickly learned that breadth was the same as width. If you read the story of David and Goliath, you see that Goliath was 6 cubits and a span. A span is about 9 inches; meaning, Goliath was 9 feet 9 inches tall. Another thing that is very important is knowing the true meaning of words. People can use words in a sentence even if they don't know what they mean. And if you read something but don't know what every word is, it can change everything.

I started reading out of a New King James Version Bible that had a glossary at the back of the book. I actually spent several hours doing nothing but memorizing the words that I didn't know. Some, I haven't used enough to remember exactly what each of them are, but I would like to point out a couple that really stuck out. For instance, the word *cherubim*, which appears very early in the Bible and is repeated throughout. That's a word I can't truthfully say I'd ever heard or remember hearing in real life. Another would be what *amen* really means.

Getting into the Bible can be hard. They have those "read the Bible in a year" reading plans, and I will never put down anyone's strategy for reading the Bible because I would never tell someone to stop reading the Bible. However, I've noticed that when you get on something like that, you're sort of holding yourself back. Having a set amount of reading that is intended to encourage someone to just read a little bit each day is almost like giving them a diet. When you are on a diet, you say you can only take in so many calories; and after that, you can't eat anymore. I've actually heard someone say they wanted to continue reading the Bible, but the only thing holding them back was that they had finished what that piece of paper said to read that day. Imagine trying to watch a movie, and every fifteen minutes, you had to pause it and take an hour break. Not only would it take you a long time to watch the movie, but it would be extremely frustrating. You'd find yourself wanting to rewind a little to refresh your memory on what had just happened.

You don't know how many times I've asked someone what they read in the Bible, and they really have no idea. So what I'm going to recommend to you is this: first, start reading small stories. I first looked for the story of David and Goliath and Samson and Delilah, two stories I was familiar with growing up. Jonah and the whale is a really short story. I'd never read that one, but when I did, I was very glad because I'd heard of it, but not necessarily the real story. I don't know which stories you've heard, but the ones you have that seem interesting are what I recommend you to start with. Then from there, definitely read all the way through Genesis. Genesis has so many stories in it that really the whole book is interesting. I'm then going to recommend you change course after reading a few chapters of Exodus because once you get into the second to the fifth books in the Bible, it begins to get really confusing and possibly boring. To avoid discouragement or losing interest, I would recommend reading up to the point where the Israelites were wandering in the wilderness but then skipping to Joshua. From there, the next three to five books should be fairly interesting.

If you begin to lose interest, at some point, skip to the New Testament, which begins with the four Gospels, then the book of acts, and then there are just several letters that are packed with great Bible verses. The book of James to me is what we should all strive for. It has such simple teachings, yet because of the way we've been conformed to this world, it seems impossible to do what he's saying.

I'm going to end this book with a small Bible study made up only of questions and answers found in the book of James.

Now I'm going to share with you something I think has helped me immensely. Just a couple months into reading the Bible, I decided I *wanted* to learn where each book in the Bible was, or more specifically, the order of the books. Don't you get tired of searching for a certain verse—someone says look up Philippians 4:13 and won't tell you what it is but hand you a Bible, and after fifteen minutes of looking for it, you give up; or your pastor says open up to this verse, and while you're still looking for it, he starts reading so you just have to stop what you're doing? Well, about seven to ten months into my Bible reading, I finally did what I'd been wanting to do: I got serious about learning the order of the books in the Bible. You can tell me any number from one to sixty-six, and I can instantly tell you what book of the Bible it is. For instance, sixteen is Nehemiah, fifty-five is 2 Timothy, fifty-three is 2 Thessalonians, thirty-nine is Malachi, seven is Judges, and so on. Sixteen months ago, I couldn't even tell you the first three books in the Bible. Learning this was one thing I'm more than glad I took the time to do. Being able to find any verse that is referenced comes in handier than you think, if you use your Bible regularly. I can't stress this enough: the more you know about the Bible, the easier understanding it becomes. Think about learning a new language. The more words you understand, the easier understanding the language becomes!

What's your favorite Bible verse? Do you know how many times I've heard someone say John 3:16, and then when I asked their second favorite verse, they couldn't even answer me because they didn't have a second verse memorized? What is your favorite Bible verse? What's your second favorite Bible verse? What's your third favorite Bible verse? If you can't answer that, I recommend you read from the book of Romans through Jude. Although some of my favorite verses do come from other books, such as Joshua 24:15, which reads something along the lines of, "As for me and my family, we will serve the Lord"; or Matthew 6:34, which reads something like, "Don't worry about tomorrow because today will bring enough worries of its own." There can be a lot of reading to pinpoint that one really meaningful verse worth memorizing.

From Romans to Jude, the verses for memorizing are much more tightly packed. And once you get past Romans and 1 and 2 Corinthians, a lot of the books are only a couple pages long, so you can set yourself a more-than-realistic goal to read a full book in one sitting and highlight meaningful verses that are worth memorizing. When you read your Bible, don't be afraid to underline meaningful verse. You'd be surprised when you look through the Bible at a later date how that verse you underlined two months earlier really sticks out to you. You are just flipping through your Bible and notice that one specific verse is underlined on a page, so you stop to read it; and from that day on, it sticks forever.

I'm now going to strongly encourage something I demonstrated in chapter 10. I've found that studying a specific man in the Bible to me is more interesting than just reading a book. I actually have begun underlining every time I read a name in Bible. But, for example, if you started with Noah in Genesis 5:28–29, you read, "And Lamech lived an hundred eighty and two years, and begat a son: and he called his name Noah." Now skip to Genesis 9:29: "And all the days of Noah were nine hundred and fifty years: and he died." So we have Noah's life from Genesis 5:28 to Genesis 9:29. Now I'll include a short list of others to get you started.

- Abraham: Genesis 11:26–25:10
- Isaac: Genesis 21:2–35:29
- Jacob: Genesis 25:26–49:33
- David: 1 Samuel 16:12–2 Samuel 2:10

If you get to a point where you don't feel you are learning a whole lot or are possibly getting bored or tired of reading, go back to some more facts that you find from reading the Bible, like for example the names of the first twelve disciples Jesus called, as well as the man who took Judas's place, which you'll find in the book of Acts. There is so much to learn, but really, all it comes down to is starting somewhere, learning enough to know what people are talking about some of the time, and knowing enough to ask questions. Don't think you have to be stuck on any certain schedule; just read. But at some point, try to get where you are reading it one book at a time, and possibly just start with the smallest books. Most Bibles include an index with each book showing how many pages are in each one. I'm not telling you *not* to read it from front to back, but what I'm saying is not reading it from front to back isn't going to make it confusing like it would be reading a regular novel just jumping around pages.

If you enjoyed my book, you can look forward to more books from me in which I'll focus on specific teachings and get more in depth. Remember, this was to serve as a map, to find out where you are in your Christian walk with God and what you need to do to get to heaven. Within each chapter, there are full books already written to help you in each of those areas.

Consider this: there are thousands of workout programs. It seems like a new program is coming out constantly, claiming a new way to get you into shape quicker or easier. I'm about to reveal the secret to getting in shape. Just work out. Just choose any of them, pick one, do it—soon you'll develop your own workout. Every person who designed a workout they are now selling started somewhere; they listened to someone else or watched someone else. The key to reading the Bible is just—start somewhere. Right now, my technique for reading the Bible is choosing a book and reading it carefully, circling every time I see the word *Lord*, *God*, or *Jesus*. I underline every name and anything I feel is important or really sticks out to me.

To me, there are two ways to read the Bible efficiently. You can either read it "slowly" or "repetitively." Personally, I choose to use the "slowly" method, but I've heard of several proven Bible readers reading the Bible front to back over and over and over. I, however, choose to read it slowly because I am really big on taking notes. Jesus told a parable about sowing seed. He said that if it's not planted efficiently, the evil one comes and takes the seed before it's able to be properly planted. I find this to be very true, but the way you overcome the evil one is by taking notes and reviewing them later to remember what you felt was very important but can no longer remember.

Chapter 17
The Compass

Before my official teachings begin, I want to get you up to speed with a few definitions that all come from the dictionary app on my Android.

Compass

- Awareness or understanding one's purpose or objectives
- To understand; comprehend
- Instrument for finding direction
- To comprehend or grasp mentally

Heaven

- Abode of God, the angels, and the soul of those who are granted salvation
- An eternal state of communion with God; everlasting bliss

HEAVEN QUEST: A DETOUR HOME

Quest

- The act or instance of seeking or pursuing something; a search

Detour

- A roundabout way or course, especially a road used temporarily instead of a main route
- A deviation from a direct course of action

Home

- A place where one lives, a residence
- A dwelling place together with the family or social unit that occupies it, a household
- An environment offering security and happiness
- A valued place, such as a refuge or place of origin
- The place where something is discovered, founded, developed, or promoted; a source

If it never made sense before, I'm hoping very soon you'll understand the title of my book. First, we have *heaven*, which is where we hope to go when we die. It's where we will spend eternity with Jesus Christ, other incredible men and women we can read about in the Bible, and our very Creator, God himself.

Next, we have *quest*, which is seeking or pursuing something. Most of us spend our lives seeking or searching for whatever will make us happy. Unfortunately, we tend to find the wrong things before we truly understand what is most important—finding happiness in the things that will lead us to heaven!

Here's the most unfortunate thing about all this: most of us take a *detour* that we never had to take. This detour takes us right down a road full of sin. When I say *we* or *us*, I'm speaking as humans in general. But not everyone takes this detour. One man who didn't seem to take a detour would be Samuel. His mother, who had no children, prayed to God for a child and promised to give him back to the Lord and to the priest to be raised in the temple. Her son grew up around religious leaders and seemed to be very obedient to God from the time of his birth to the time of his death. But we have many more examples of people who, in fact, did take a detour to sin.

Something that wasn't exactly pointed out in my *detour* definition is the fact that when a detour ends, it doesn't mean you are at your destination; it just means that you are simply back on a road that directly leads to your desired location. After we fall to the disobedience of the first time we do something wrong—whether it be using profound language, starting a tobacco addiction, gambling, doing drugs and alcohol, committing sexual sins, whatever it may be (and for many of us, it's not just one)—we, at some point, begin what becomes a struggle or journey to overcome it.

I pointed out that, usually, the first time we disobey something, it's possible it wasn't exactly our own idea, but instead we were deceived by someone or something. We then begin to enjoy it and want it so bad that nothing would stop us from it. Sometimes the way that we are deceived is actually just by watching or following in someone else's footsteps whom we didn't believe would lead us astray.

We then become a leader in sin if we don't immediately stop at the time the sinning began. At the time you became a leader in sin, you caused a detour in someone else's life. You kept the sin cycle alive. The first five chapters of my book are a vicious cycle in which there is no guarantee that someone will realize they are at the wrong destination before it's too late. Consider someone who dies of a drug overdose or during a drunken driving accident—they were at the wrong destination but never got the chance to change direction.

The most unfortunate thing in the world today is when someone wants to change but doesn't know how. I began a small study on why there are so many parentless children. It became very apparent to me that most bad parents grew up without good parents. This told me that they simply didn't know how to be a good parent because they had never been taught. I once heard a man who had lost custody of his son say that he always vowed that he would be a good father because he grew up without a good father and said he'd never do that to his son. He ended up exactly like his father anyway, and the reason is very simple. He was watching his father closely as he walked in and out of his life, and he uncontrollably learned how to be just like him.

The problem with starting your life over in a new manner is you become you because of the people in your life. Regardless of what people who love to tell someone to stop hanging around a certain crowd think, it's not always that simple. I myself went through a time in my life where I wanted to stop hanging around the "wrong crowd." This would be the bar goers, gamblers, and other public sinners. What I found was that anyone I considered a friend who wasn't out sinning openly was at home raising a family. That left me in a situation where I had to choose between being alone and being with the wrong people. Who wants to be alone?

The way I overcome that alone time that I let devour me once before is by turning to the Bible. You have to learn how to live in a different way, but in most cases, finding a living, breathing human mentor can be very hard. When I found myself in a position where I was crying out for help because I wanted out of the life I seemed to be trapped in, I asked a pastor to speak with me. Before I really got anything out of the conversation, he looked at his watch and told me he had to go. My Bible has never closed without my own hands causing it to. I'd like to believe that anything that Pastor was going to teach me would have come from the Bible.

Once you begin reading the Bible, whether you are already attending church or not, the Bible should help you realize that Sunday church is not enough. I grew up Catholic, where they had a Saturday night service and two Sunday services. It was my parents' goal to get us to one of the three. The first church I found myself settled in after I was born again had a service on Wednesday, as well as two on Sunday. I heard someone say that the Wednesday service is a chance to "recharge your batteries." I don't know about you, but the only thing that I have to constantly charge to keep working properly is my phone. And if I tried to charge my phone only once or twice a week, it wouldn't work five or six days out of the week. The way you "keep your batteries charged" is by engaging in the Word of God daily. Once you begin to do that, you'll truly understand why Sunday church definitely is not enough.

> Once you finally realize that Sunday church isn't enough, it starts a whole new journey, the journey you'll be on once you accept Paul's words from Romans 15:1. This will include many things such as failures and hardships. I only included two very important tips to help you understand what it will take. Chapters 13 and 14 are my way of telling you it will take *effort* and *love*. Anyone can show up and go to church. People go to church and cry over the sins they've committed but walk right out the door and do it again. I'm not saying it's impossible, but it's definitely much less common that someone who is doing more outside of church is still showing up to church in that manner.

Getting that ticket to heaven is actually more reliant on your life outside church than the fact that you do in fact make it to church. It seems like prior to junior high school, certain teachers had some type of little reward system. Whenever they saw someone do some special, out-of-the-ordinary act of kindness, they could hand you a little certificate or a sticker to show that you did something special. Everyone who was at school could have gotten one, but only the ones doing something extra special actually did get one. The kid who missed school that day because of a sickness was the only one who didn't have a chance to receive a reward that day. But not everyone who was at school got the special reward.

The most important thing I could ever try to teach someone is how to read the Bible. The Bible has the capabilities of preparing you for any situation in life. Knowing how to connect the problems men faced in the Bible with the problems we face today is the key to it all.

I was reading the Bible with a young man almost daily. I thought he was really learning a lot; he always came back, asking if I was ready for Bible study. One day, he finally asked me this question, "How do I use this in my life?" I was actually very surprised at this question. I had been filling him with Bible "knowledge," but I realized that he was still very much lacking wisdom. I believe that knowledge is "knowing something," and wisdom is" knowing how to use it." I didn't know how to make him understand what I was trying to teach him. Finally, I just had to explain it like this:

Picture this: there is a man who comes across a box. The box is very unique, and it's completely enclosed. It seems to be hollow but unbreakable and shows no sign of how its sides are being held together. This mysterious wooden box is said to contain all the secrets in the world, but the only problem is, nobody knows how to use it. The man finally comes across a great shaman, whose only advice to the man was, "When you're ready to use it, you'll know how to use it." That was my advice to that young man.

It also sort of made sense because I had recently heard that thirty is the age of spiritual maturity. It has been backed up by facts such as Joseph being thirty years old when he became second-in-command only to Pharaoh. Thirty and upward is said to be the age in which men should enter the priesthood. David was thirty when he became king, and John and Jesus were both thirty when they began their ministry. The young man I was working with was only twenty-one years old, so I simply encouraged him to continue to gain Bible knowledge and that someday it would all make sense.

The Bible tells many stories about humans of the past. The Bible is said to be a compilation of books that tell a single story. *Heaven Quest* was designed to tell the story of my journey in life. Although my life has been uniquely put together by various events that, as a whole, will differ from any other human in existence, other people will share the same struggles.

This book may not mean anything to a lot of people in the world, but I believe I'm not the only one who has experienced the things that inspired me to write this book. I believe I'm back on the right road that will lead to heaven, but I didn't get here without taking a major detour first.

Even after making it back on the right road once before, I ended up taking another major detour. Luke 11:24–25 reads:

> When an unclean spirit goes out of a man, he goes through dry places, seeking rest; and finding none, he says, 'I will return to my house from which I came.' "And when he comes, he finds it swept and put in order. "Then he goes and takes with him seven other spirits more wicked than himself, and they enter and dwell there; and the last state of that man is worse than the first. (NKJV)

I want to make something very clear to everyone. I've heard before that once you're truly born again, you never return to your old life. One day, I decided to look up the difference between Methodist and Baptist church beliefs. One thing that really stuck out to me was one believed that once you're saved, you're always saved; and the other believed you could fall from salvation. This really troubled me. I actually began to believe that since I had been saved and returned to my old life, I had no chance of making it to heaven. I then began to believe that since I was already "born again," I was automatically going to heaven no matter what I did the rest of my life. Once I had both thoughts, I was more confused than ever. Finally, the Holy Spirit made this very clear to me: you can be born again and still end up in hell, but getting to heaven will be even easier because the Holy Spirit will guide you. Once you've made the decision to spend eternity in heaven, there is one more thing you may or may not care to consider: Where do you want to sit?

PS: Earlier, I mentioned that we don't know what exactly Noah was doing that was so pleasing to God. I want to point one thing out about Noah. This is what it says about Noah after God gave him multiple instructions. Genesis 6:22 reads,

Thus Noah did; according to all that God commanded him, so he did.

CPSIA information can be obtained
at www.ICGtesting.com
Printed in the USA
FSOW01n1345010717
35715FS